How the word became flesh

Story dramas
for worship
and religious education

by Michael Moynahan

ISBN 0-89390-029-X.
Library of Congress Catalog Card Number 80-54874.

Acknowledgements:
Cover design and book layout: George F. Collopy
Typography: Nancy MacMorran
Production: Stephen Weikart

Published by Resource Publications, Inc., P. O. Box 444, Saratoga, CA 95070. Printed and bound in the United States of America 4 3 2 1.

Foreword

Michael Moynahan has given us a book of prayer and theology. Although as the subtitle indicates, it is a collection of story dramas for education and worship, a careful reading of these scripts or even better, a live experience of these dramatizations in the sanctuary or classroom reveals that here we have both an alternate form of theological articulation as well as creative ways of proclamation. In either case what appears to be a mere collection of stories is in fact a rich resource exemplifying how the human imagination is a contemporary font for enlivening both liturgical worship and theological education.

What Michael Moynahan is doing in *How The Word Became Flesh* is assisting the Christian worshipper and educator to rediscover the power of images. Often in the past our teaching has been too cerebral and even the recently reformed Roman Catholic liturgy lives under the dominance of the intellectual. Happily, today our sources for religious education and liturgy are more clearly understandable and less cluttered. But they are still too discursive and textual. The explosive power of the symbolic is lacking. This loss of symbolic reality is at the heart of the failure of the contemporary liturgical movement. Clear language and more cogent structure have not led to a more engaging experience of transcendence. Often our new worship is addressed to only a part of the human person. It is not a liturgy which takes the human body, feelings and emotions seriously. It treats the worshipper as some kind of "disembodied spirit." And to the sobriety of the former Roman Rite we have added the criterion of functionality. Thus, while the rites are reformed, the ritual is not renewed because the symbols are explained or described rather than being freshly experienced in the human imagination.

For the liturgy today this means a new crisis, not one of texts, structures and historical continuity, but one of spirituality. Faith is expressed and effectively celebrated in symbols that have their rootage in the imagination. But reformed liturgical formulas are still offering explanations rather than setting up a resonance in the worshipper by means of imaging. Our overly conceptual liturgy is better at communicating doctrinal affirmations than it is in engaging us in a relationship which points to the transcendent. Just as theological propositions do not necessarily lead to religious commitment, so a liturgy devoid of images, which connect the conscious and unconscious dimensions of human life, is impotent for producing awe and mystery. Belief in God which is the grounding of our experience of transcendence begins in image and symbol more than in concepts. In liturgy the reality of God should be redescribed and presented in a way that is different from the more conceptual modes of communication. In other words, liturgy must be a metaphor.

How The Word Became Flesh can help restore the metaphorical character to public praise. The engagement called for through the kinds of imagining found in these dramas can once again give worship that disclosive power which distinguishes it from the classroom. There is an immediacy about the dramatic experience that stirs the imagination and the creative powers of people. It gives the worshipper ready access and direct availability to the symbolic experience.

For many the question at once arises about confusing liturgy and theater. While the two remain distinct media, worship can learn much from the dramatic experience and precisely in the area one would least expect: congregational participation. In the dramatic presentation the response of the audience is essential to the final definition of the event. Members of the audience know that they are important, that they are indispensable. In the very moment that their presence is presupposed, they are confronted by the dramatic action with a call to faith. The theater audience is asked to believe. Good dramas should be no more pedagogical or didactic than good liturgy. Like worship theater is an invitation to contemplation by means of images, events, actions and characters. Individuals enjoying a play are challenged to explore the deepest meaning of the characters within the context of their personal histories. The audience must enter into an imaginative relationship with these characters and eventually discern the effects of these interactions on their lives. The kind of understanding that results from the dramatic experience enables one to embrace the contemplation of one's humanity with new insights and to rededicate one's life to the growth process.

Is liturgy any different in this regard? The congregation is equally indispensable to the liturgical action. It is the faith of the worshippers which renders the liturgy truthful and valid. In worship each Christian as well as the community as a whole are invited to contemplate their relationship with God through the images mobilized by the Christian symbols, the major events and characters of salvation history and the actions of Christ in the past and in the community in the present. The liturgy is the place where the history of each Christian is caught up in the larger incorporating story of Jesus Christ.

On one level in both liturgy and drama there is make-believe and pretending. Both live by the power of their myths. But their myths are true. In liturgy the Christian myths are mediated by

2

dramatic images and so they become visible. Through liturgical drama we can touch the imperceptible. Jesus Christ, the Word made flesh, becomes a living metaphor in dramatic proclamation. To participate in this root metaphor through worship is to be transformed. Through the imaginative process the believers image Christ and so are caught up into the movement of salvation. And so, just as the theater audience can be transformed by a belief which moves the heart to hope and care for the people on the stage which in turn can lead to a greater human sharing, the Christian assembly can experience such transformation in their ritual. *How The Word Became Flesh* offers the Christian liturgist an opportunity to recapture these imaginative aspects of the dramatic experience which empower ritual to achieve its true sacramental purpose.

The theater can serve as a model for good liturgy because it is still the place where people are invited to enter and express themselves in depth by creating a world more human than their ordinary one, by suspending disbelief to live by a secular faith, and by participating and so losing themselves in the experience of others. As one must hand oneself over to the aesthetic experience, in this case, the actors on the stage, so in good worship one is required to abandon oneself in community to the images which the Church has used to mediate the Paschal Mystery.

Theologian, David Tracy, in his *Blessed Rage for Order* has convincingly argued for the need for more than conceptual analysis to understand human existence. Human beings need images, stories and fictions so that their imaginations may explode with new possibilities. He says: "Fictions do not operate to help us escape reality, but to redescribe our human reality in such disclosive terms that we return to the 'everyday' reoriented to life's real — if forgotten or sometimes never even imagined — possibilities" (p. 207). Tracy calls for drama to open our minds, our imaginations and our hearts so that we might be transformed in our liturgical worship. Michael Moynahan has shown us how to do it.

James L. Empereur, S.J.

TABLE OF CONTENTS

The Story Dramatizations

Preface

At the heart of our christian spirituality is the Word of God. This Word creates us. It calls us together to journey in community. It finds us when we are lost. It heals us when we are wounded. It nourishes us when we are hungry. It renews us when we are weary. It reminds us when we forget.

God has spoken to us. This is the beginning and foundation of our Biblical faith. God has proclaimed love for us in creation, in exodus, in redemption, in Jesus Christ. God's Word speaks to all the seasons and experiences of our lives: beginnings and endings, strength and weakness, belief and unbelief, doubt and hope, and the countless other faces of life and death.

Throughout history God has spoken in many ways. God speaks through men and women, prophets, paupers, the learned and the lowly. People have discovered that God's love has many appearances. Some have sung of God's love. Others have danced God's love. Jesus told stories of God's love. Paul wrote letters about it. Early prophets even mimed God's love. There is no one simple all-encompassing way to proclaim God's love because that love knows no bounds.

God continues to speak to us, to move our hearts, by speaking to us in ways that allow us to hear and respond. God's Word became flesh in Jesus. When God spoke to Jesus, some people were scandalized while others found hope. Modern day attempts to proclaim the Word of God as effectively as possible should not expect more success than God experienced.

God spoke to us in former days by utilizing the gifts of those who spoke of this love. Sometimes the gift was song. Other times it was mime or dance. Still other times it was story. I come from a mother who loved the stage and a father who loved to tell stories. Little wonder, then, that the best way I have found to speak of God's mysterious and ever-present love is through story dramas.

Had these dramas not been well received, had they not led people to experience the Word of God in new and powerful ways, had they not bound the communities they served together in prayer, I would have been disappointed but I would still have written them. They are the way that I understand and can proclaim the love that has given me life and breath and direction on this marvelous adventure called life. This love and this life cannot be bottled up. It is infectious and must be shared.

There are three major influences on each of these story dramas.

Each dramatization was created for a specific occasion. They were not created in a vacuum. A liturgical feast or season occasioned the creation of each dramatization. It called for something special, something more. It was the occasion of our creativity.

The second important influence on each dramatization was the congregation with which we celebrated. If these liturgical dramas had been sprung on a totally unsuspecting and unprepared community, they might have been retitled "liturgical traumas." In each case, I accepted invitations from communities that were looking for newer and fuller ways to proclaim the Word of God and respond to it.

In each case, it was important to listen to the needs and hopes of that particular community. Wherever possible, representatives of each community were included in the faith-sharing, brainstorming and creative process. Members of the respective congregations worked with members of the Berkeley Liturgical Drama Guild (BLDG) to enact and proclaim these story dramatizations to their respective communities.

The third major influence on each dramatization was the ministers. There were the special ministers of each congregation who had carefully listened to the needs of their people and looked for help in more effectively proclaiming God's Word to them. And there were the members of BLDG who are all special ministers of the Word. It was the combination of all these influences that shaped each liturgical dramatization in this volume.

Now what are you to do with these story dramas? Read them. Enjoy them. Let them touch you. Let them spark your own religious imagination. Let them suggest countless possibilities and settings. They are appropriate for use in the classroom. Everyone loves a story. Use them to help your students dive into the mysterious depths and richness of the Word of God. They are appropriate for worship. Everyone loves a story. Just think of Jesus pulling rich and poor alike into the experience of God's love through good stories. If your community or congregation is open to this type of proclamation, find some special occasion on which you can proclaim God's Word through drama. It can and does work when well done.

But don't stop here. These are just models, examples of what liturgical dramas might look like. Why not try to create some of your own? How would your family or class or congregation allow the Word to become flesh in the 1980's? In attempting to create story dramas, we are attempting to allow the Word of God to illumine our lives and experience. This Word of God needs to be proclaimed freshly in each generation, in each congregation.

Finally, some precautions are in order. Creating liturgical dramas takes time, creativity and energy. It demands commitment and dedication. If you expect to whip up a story dramatization in a few hours, I suggest that you abandon the project. Each of the dramas in this book represents eight hours (four two-hour sessions) of faith-sharing, brain-storming and imaginative creating, as well as at least four hours (two two-hour sessions) of rehearsal. The Word of God we proclaim and the congregations we serve deserve our dedication. It is this type of seriousness or reverence for the Word of God that can call forth the same such reverence and commitment from our classrooms and congregations.

Strive to be simple in your story dramas. There should be a theme, a focus to each of your story dramas. What is that focus in one sentence? Don't allow your story dramas to wander and become tangential. Let them lift up the Word of God in all its simplicity and power. Children of all ages should be able to follow them and enter into them fully.

Strive to be clear in your story dramas. Does your story drama proclaim the Good News of Scripture? Does it do what you intended it to do? If it is contrived or muddled, it will be ineffective.

And finally, strive to be brief in your story dramas. Many homilists are guilty of trying to cover all of salvation history in each of their homilies. This will spell disaster for your liturgical dramatic efforts. These liturgical dramas were all originally done as acted-out homilies. Each of the dramas in this book is intended to be performed in fifteen to twenty minutes. Practice and precision will allow you to stay within these limits.

Some thanks are in order. I am grateful to Jake Empereur, SJ, who first asked a fledgling theological student with some background in drama to create a liturgical drama for a Holy Week celebration back in 1971. This was the beginning. I am deeply grateful to Don Osuna and the worshippers of St. Francis De Sales Cathedral in Oakland, CA, for giving me and liturgical drama a home. This was the deepening. And I am particularly grateful to five Jesuits who asked me in 1976 to work with them. Together with me they founded the Berkeley Liturgical Drama Guild. They are J-Glenn Murray, George Murry, Jack Fagan, John McConville, and Rick Sistek. This was the flowering.

To these and all those who have swelled BLDG'S ranks and helped create these liturgical dramas, to the churches and congregations that have opened their doors and hearts to us, to all of those who cherish the Word of God and strive to let it be proclaimed and take flesh in our day and age, to all of you I gratefully dedicate this book.

Michael E. Moynahan, SJ
Jesuit School of Theology
Berkeley, CA

A Dragon Tamed Is A Friend Forever

Cast:	The Mayor	The Town Crier
	The Carpenter	The Dragon
	The Tailor	The Stranger
	The Blacksmith	The Narrator
	The Bartender	The Nurse
	The Teacher	

Narrator: Once upon a time, in a far off distant land, there was a small town where everyone lived in peace and harmony. The townspeople were so peaceful and so tranquil that they named their town Peaceful Village.

Now in Peaceful Village there were many wonderful people. Among the townspeople there was a Mayor, a carpenter, a tailor, and a blacksmith. And these were not all. There were many other townspeople as well. And they all lived and worked happily together.

But then, one day, chaos came to Peaceful Village.

Crier: CHAOS IS COMING!

All: Chaos? Chaos? Chaos?

Crier: I mean the DRAGON IS COMING!

All: The DRAGON! *(General pandamonium follows.)*

Narrator: Now this threw the townsfolk into utter confusion. The lovely little townspeople of Peaceful Village could not believe their ears. There was only one thing on this whole wide earth that could possibly destroy their peace and tranquility, and that was HERMAN THE HUMONGOUS DRAGON! *(Herman enters to appropriate dragon music. The theme from Peer Gynt is suggested. When the dragon reaches the sanctuary, he growls or roars at the townspeople and they are frightened.)*

Herman lived in a dark, dank cave, deep in the mountains of Doom. From time to time, he would journey to one of the nearby villages and perform all sorts of mischief on the terrified townspeople. Today was Peaceful Village's unlucky day!

Herman was big, and mean, and ugly, and worst of all, he had bad breath! After Herman had made his way through Peaceful Village pillaging and breaking anything he could get his claws on, romping and stomping on everything in sight, he went to the edge of town for a deep dragon sleep after a full day of mischief.

When Herman was gone, the frightened villagers called an emergency town meeting. The Mayor was the first to speak.

Mayor: Well, I guess you all know why I called you here?

All: Yeah!

Mayor: We have a problem, and he weighs about two tons.

All: Yeah!

Mayor: Now how do we get rid of an ornery two ton dragon?

All: Yeah? How do we get rid of one?

Narrator: So, the people thought very hard and very long. Finally, the Mayor spoke up.

Mayor: I've got an idea! Did any of you ever hear the story of St. George and the dragon?

All: Yeah!

Mayor: Well, why don't we get someone to go slay that dastardly dragon with a sword?

All: Yeah!

Mayor: O.K., then, any volunteers? I said any volunteers?

Nurse: Why don't you do it? It's your idea!

All: Yeah!

Mayor: All in favor of me, signify your assent by saying "aye". *(Everyone says "aye" except the Mayor.)* All opposed, signify your dissent by saying "nay". *(The Mayor says "nay".)* Well, the "ayes" have it. Alright, if that's the way you feel, I'll be St. George. But remember, you may not have me to kick around as Mayor anymore!

Narrator:	And so, the Mayor, sword in hand, went out and confronted the dragon who had fallen into a deep sleep. *(The dragon wakes up and destroys the sword. The Mayor runs back to town and the villagers register their disappointment.)* But the Mayor forgot that he wasn't really St. George, only a Mayor. And so, his plan failed.
	Next, the carpenter spoke up.
Carpenter:	I've got an idea! I saw a John Wayne movie one time in which he fought off a whole gang of desperadoes single-handedly.
All:	How'd he do that?
Carpenter:	He liquored them all up! He got them so drunk that they couldn't see what they were doing or whom to shoot at!
All:	Great idea!
Carpenter:	So, give me my hat *(Puts on hat.)*, my trusty six-shooter *(Puts on holster and six-shooter.)*, and the booze *(Takes a large cutout bottle with BOOZE written across it.)*. I'll fix that dragon's wagon! *(As the carpenter departs, the villagers hum "Do not forsake me Oh my darlin'.')*
Narrator:	And so the carpenter went out to meet the dragon.
Carpenter:	O.K., dragon, this town ain't big enough for both of us. It's you or me! And I say it's you! So get ready to meet your maker, dragon! 'Cause I'm gonna fill you so full of holes that you could pass for a big piece of swiss cheese! But just to show there's no hard feelin's, why don't you have one short snort for the road. *(The dragon roars.)* No, I mean one drink!
Dragon:	Maybe poison. You drink first.
Carpenter:	O.K. Here! *(During the dragon's next lines, the carpenter keeps trying to offer the bottle to him.)*
Dragon:	No! Drink again! And again! And again! And again!
Carpenter:	*(Turning to the congregation drunk.)* O.K. dragon, go for it! Where are you, dragon? No use hiding! *(The carpenter turns.)* Oh, there you are. Well, reach for it! (The dragon hits the carpenter into the arms of the townspeople. They sigh.)

Narrator:	But the carpenter forgot that he wasn't John Wayne, only a carpenter. And so, his plan failed. The people were nervous now. They were running out of time and ideas. As a matter of fact, they were down to their last plan.
	So, the tailor spoke up.
Tailor:	Wait a minute! Wait a minute! I don't think the dragon even exists!
All:	What?
Tailor:	I think he's just a figment of our imaginations!
All:	What? What?
Tailor:	Yeah! You know, when you're suffering from something just in your head, they call it psychosomatic. So the dragon is psychosomatic!
All:	What?
Tailor:	That's right! If we convince ourselves he isn't real, he'll cease to exist!
All:	No way!
Tailor:	Alright, I'll prove it to you. It's all right here in this little book entitled "Reasoning Away Your Worries" by Eric Von Slop.
Narrator:	So, the gallant little tailor made his way out to confront the dragon, armed only with his new knowledge. But a little knowledge is dangerous. *(The tailor knocks on the dragon's door. He proceeds to deny the dragon's existence as the dragon gets madder and madder. Finally the dragon picks up the tailor and shakes him. The tailor runs back to the villagers and shouts:)*
Tailor:	He's real! He's real!
Narrator:	But the tailor forgot that he was no Eric Von Slop, just a simple tailor. So, his plan failed too. The last hope of Peaceful Village was dashed that afternoon. The townspeople despaired! The dragon survived and grew more vile and mischievous with each passing day. He would come into town on occasion and terrorize the helpless inhabitants.
	Then one day, a stranger came into town playing a happy little melody on his flute. This disturbed and puzzled the inhabitants of Peaceful Village, because they no longer found anything to be happy

about. Finally, one of the villagers asked the stranger:

Bartender: Hey, why are you playing that happy song on your dumb flute?

Stranger: Because it's a beautiful day and there's so much to be happy about.

All: No, there isn't! Not here, at least!

Stranger: What do you mean?

Teacher: For the past three years we have been living in constant fear of Herman the Humongous Dragon. Now he lives on the outskirts of town ready to pounce on us at any moment.

Stranger: Have you tried to get rid of him?

Nurse: We've tried everything! We tried to be St. George, and that didn't work. Someone tried to be John Wayne, but that didn't work either. Finally, someone tried to be Eric Von Slop, but that failed too. Nothing worked! We are helpless now!

Stranger: Oh, my friends, you have been going about this thing all wrong.

All: What do you mean?

Stranger: You can't be someone else. The only way you can tame a dragon is to be your best self!

All: Oh go on! *(Disbelief.)*

Stranger: Yes, my friends, you can do it if you are willing to be your best selves. Do you want to try?

Mayor: Well, what have we got to lose? Things can't get any worse!

Narrator: And so, the townspeople were overwhelmed by the gentleness, the courage and strength of the young stranger. He spoke with authority. He told them they must be their best selves to meet and tame the dragon, so the inhabitants of Peaceful Village spent the next weeks preparing to be their best selves. They struggled to be more honest with each other. They began not only to smile at one another but to grow in patience and love. They discovered what understanding and forgiveness were all about. Through all this they learned what real peace was all about.

Finally, when they were ready, they followed the stranger out of town to meet the dragon. It was a classic confrontation. When the people got there, the dragon roared. *(Dragon roars.)* And the people quaked. *(The people shiver in fear.)* But the stranger told them:

Stranger: Have faith! Don't be afraid! Believe in me! Believe in your best selves! Just remember what I told you! *(Here the dragon roars and the people don't budge. The villagers move toward him and finally say:)*

All: Boo!

Narrator: And so the dragon began to cry because he knew that the people, from this day forward, would never be afraid of him again. The townspeople were ready to give the dragon a little of his own medicine when the stranger stopped them.

Stranger: Don't be too hard on the dragon. Repay his rudeness and mischief with kindness. In this way you can tame him with your love and understanding. And everyone knows that a dragon tamed is a friend forever. *(Villagers gradually accept the dragon.)*

Narrator: Oh what rejoicing and merriment there was in Peaceful Village that day! Everyone thanked the stranger.

All: Thanks, stranger!

Narrator: But as the celebration continued, the stranger began to make his way out of town. When the people noticed this they stopped and yelled to him.

Nurse: Hey, stranger, where are you going?

Stranger: To other towns and villages.

Crier: But why are you leaving us?

Stranger: Because there are other people who need me. Because they too are burdened with dragons they don't know how to tame!

Mayor: But what will we do next time a dragon comes to town?

All: Yes, what will we do? What will we do?

Stranger: I will leave you the Book of Heroes, Sheroes and other Saints. When you have a dragon to confront, simply open the book. Look deeply into it. The

14

book will reveal to you who you are to be when you meet your next dragon. So, go ahead, open it up! All of you, open the book and see. Look long and deeply and remember what you have seen and what you have heard. This is how you meet your dragons. *(They all open the little books and discover.)*

Narrator: And now a reading from the Book of Heroes, Sheroes and other Saints. *(Here the Gospel can be read.)*

Finis

Theme: Heroes, Sheroes and Other Saints.

Scripture: John 17:14-19. *(Your Word is truth.)*, or Ephesians 3:14-21. *(May love be the root and foundation of your life.)*

Props: 1. One large sword — cut it out of cardboard or poster board and cover it with aluminum foil.

2. One Western hat.

3. One holster and six-shooter.

4. One large bottle — cut out of cardboard with "BOOZE" written across it.

5. One book — preferably a large one that can act as Eric Von Slop's volume entitled "Reasoning Away Your Worries."

6. Numerous little books of "Heroes, Sheroes and Other Saints" — there should be one of these for every member of the congregation. These are simply heavy white paper 4 ¼ inches x 11 inches folded in two. Printed on the outside of the front is "The Book of Heroes, Sheroes and other Saints." Inside there is a piece of reflective material so that the person will see their own face when they open up the "book" and look deeply into it. This little "book" should be sealed shut so that the congregation will not open it until the appropriate time in the dramatization.

Production Notes: This dramatization was originally performed at the Oakland Cathedral during their summer liturgy series entitled "Heroes, Sheroes and Other Saints." In this dramatization, as well as a number of other story-dramas in this volume, I was working with

15

Jesuit novices. Consequently, most of the roles call for a male. Men or women can play the roles. The tailor could become the seamstress, and so on. Adjust the text so that the gender of the pronouns fits the gender of the person playing the role. The script itself gives you many directorial clues. The gestures and movements you do can be as simple or elaborate as you wish. Remember to always use your imagination.

You can play the dragon any way that you would like. Create a dragon costume for the occasion. In the original production, the dragon was played by a large person wearing a green T-shirt with a big dragon on it.

Should the celebrant participate in these story-dramas if they are used in a worship context? I was generally the presider at all of the liturgies in which these story-dramas were used. I took the part of the narrator or teller of the story. This does not mean that the celebrant must take this role. That decision would be up to the worship design team (do they want the celebrant to take part in the liturgical drama?) and the celebrant (would he/she feel comfortable doing this?).

Because the narrator has such a large part of the story, his/her role can be read. The rest of the characters should memorize their lines.

Study Questions:

1. What does the dragon represent to you? What are the dragons in your life?

2. How do you deal with your dragons? Do you try to be someone else? Why?

3. Who is the Stranger? Do people wander into your life at times and help you deal with difficult situations? How?

4. What does it mean to be your best self? How do you learn to be your best self? Do the gospels give us any clues as to how we can be our best selves? What are some of those clues?

5. What do you think the villagers had to do in order to prepare to meet the dragon? Was it easy? Was it important and worthwhile?

6. Why does the stranger urge the villagers to tame rather than kill the dragon?

7. What do the villagers see when they look deeply into the Book of Heroes, Sheroes and Other Saints? What do you see?

8. What are the common ordinary ways we are called each day to become heroes, sheroes and saints? Is it possible? Is it easy? Is it important or worthwhile?

Masks

Cast: Hunter   Gerald Jock

Animal   Stanley Noseinbook

God   Upton Downer

Saint   Lorenzo Greasely

Devil   Fagan Quagmire

Angel   Injured Person

Woman   Narrator

Bandit   Burglar

Lone Ranger

Narrator: From the beginning of time, masks have played an important role in the history of peoples of the world. The inventiveness of men and women, as well as their creativity, have helped them discover a variety of uses for these masks. People have used them for playful disguising in masquerades and at carnival time. Others have used the mask for dramatic effect or characterization in the ballet, the theatre and the film. People have also discovered how to use the mask as a means of protection in sports, in industry, in war and in the game called life.

Paintings crudely etched on stone walls record the earliest use of the mask. People used them in ritual hunting dances. The first cavepeople believed that by dressing up as the hunter and the hunted and reenacting a successful "search and destroy" mission by the caveperson of his or her prey, that the real hunt would be blessed with good fortune the next day.

(Here two actors — one dressed as the animal and the other as the hunter — mime the ritual hunting dance. The hunter sights the animal. She/he takes an arrow from her/his quiver, draws the bow back and shoots the animal. The animal is hit, swoons and dies. The hunter goes over and puts the animal over her/his shoulders and carries the animal off. The actors then freeze and resume their original positions.)

Of course the ritual masking dance acted out before the hunt did not always guarantee success on the real hunt.

(Here the two actors mime the hunt again. This time the hunter sights the animal, draws an arrow from the quiver, shoots the animal. This time the animal does not swoon but turns annoyed. The animal pulls the arrow out, walks over to the hunter who looks very embarrassed. The animal winds up and delivers a windmill punch to the hunter. The hunter swoons and is carried off stage by the animal over his/her shoulder.)

Narrator: During the Medieval times, masks were used by people to depict God, angels, saints and devils in their ongoing battle for souls and power in the world.

(Here four actors hold stick masks in front of their faces. One is God who watches all of the struggle. Another is a saint who is the object of the struggle. A third is the devil who is one of the combatants. The fourth is an angel who is the other combatant. The devil and the angel play tug of war with the arms of the saint. Finally the devil puts a hand up in a gesture to stop the wrestling.)

Devil: Why don't we just flip a coin? Heads I win. Tails you lose!

(The angel looks confused. While she/he scratches her/his head, the devil pokes her/him in the angelic derriere with a pitchfork. The angel turns around with a clenched fist. God raises a hand of admonition towards the angel and indicates the angel should pray. The angel prays. God smiles on this and takes from behind her/his back a giant hammer which she/he clunks on the devil's head. The devil wanders off the stage dazed while the angel escorts the saint and God off the stage the other way.)

Narrator: Masks have always been used in literature as a means of concealment. Masks could conceal the identities of those doers of public good, those righters of wrong, those friends of the friendless. The list is long and includes such fictional greats as Batman and Robin, Wonder Woman, the Green Hornet, Captain America and the Lone Ranger.

20

(Three actors appear on stage. One is dressed as an old Western woman with a purse. One is a bandit. The third is the Lone Ranger.)

Bandit: O.K., Lady, hand over the purse or it's curtains!

Woman: Oh dear me, what can I do? Is there no one to stop this infraction of justice? *(The bandit grabs her purse and starts going through it.)*

Ranger: Pardon me, Mr. Pardoner, but is that purse yours? Or does it not, in fact, belong to the little lady? *(The bandit looks "caught in the act" and gives the purse to the Lone Ranger who in turn gives it to the lady.)*

Woman: Oh, how can I ever thank you, masked man? You sweet Ranger, you!

Ranger: No need to thank me, ma'am. It's all part of my job. *(The Lone Ranger mounts his horse and starts to go.)*

Woman: But I don't even know your name.

Ranger: Here, I think this will tell you all you need to know. *(The Lone Ranger hands her a silver bullet.)*

Woman: A masked man handing out silver bullets!

(All the characters freeze as the narrator continues the narration.)

Narrator: Masks were also used in literature to conceal the identities of villains, those dastardly doers of devilment and destruction.

(The actors come alive and are joined by a burglar wearing a mask and a taxicab hat.)

Burglar: O.K. Grandma, put the goodies in the container here. And what do we have here, Mr. Costume Ball of 1833? O.K. masked man, put the precious pellets into my brown paper bag! *(The Lone Ranger forks over all his silver bullets. The characters freeze for a moment and then leave the stage.)*

Narrator: Contemporary men and women have developed an entirely new use for the mask. Actually it is a misuse of the mask. People have become expert in fashioning the psychological mask. They use it to distance themselves from any real experience of life. They use it to conceal their real thoughts, their real feelings, their real identity.

21

In order to allow you to view first-hand the use of such masks, we take you now to a typical high school somewhere in the desperate state of confusion. Its name is Bobadilla College Prep. It is the home of the famous Bobadilla Burgers whose mascot is the Big Mac.

(A young person who has been obviously battered and wounded wanders onto the stage in a tattered shirt. She/he reaches out for help pleadingly to the congregation. Then she/he collapses on the stage. In comes Gerald Jock.)

Narrator: Please meet Gerald Jock.

(Gerald wanders in. The injured person raises a hand for help and Gerald addresses her/him.)

Gerald: Listen you whimp, up and at 'em! I've been hurt worse than you at times, but it never stopped me! If you wanted to get up you could. 'Cause when the going gets tough, the tough get going!

(Gerald turns away from the injured person and in a more natural voice says:)

I'd really like to help. But what would people think? What would they say?

(Gerald walks upstage and freezes.)

Narrator: Please meet Stanley Noseinbook.

(Stanley wanders in reading a book. Stanley trips over the injured person. The injured person reaches up for help. Stanley muses.)

Stanley: It says here that if your brain were ensconced in a vermin's sinistrel tear duct it would gyrate comparable to a sphere of minute dimensions in a reliquary preambulator!

(Stanley turns away from the injured person and in a more natural voice says:)

I'd really like to help. But what would people think? What would they say?

(Stanley walks upstage and freezes.)

Narrator: Meet Upton Downer.

(Upton wanders in with beads, a mock rolled joint. When Upton sees the injured person reaching out for help, he stops.)

Upton:	Hey man, WOW, what happened? Must have been a wild party last night! Far out! Hey man, what's the action? Oh, man, I'd love to relate, but like we're on different planets! Sorry man, I just can't cope. Later, man!
	(Upton turns aside and says in a different voice:)
	I'd really like to help. But what would people think? What would they say?
	(Upton walks upstage and freezes.)
Narrator:	Meet Lorenzo Greasely.
	(Lorenzo wanders onto the stage combing his hair. He is very neatly dressed. The injured person reaches out to him.)
Lorenzo:	Listen, nurd-head, you are in Nothin'sville! What are you doing on the ground? It's hot hot hot down there. Get up here with me and the birds in the trees, where the air is thin and if you're cool you win! Nothing's happening on the ground, clod! It's all happening up here!
	(Lorenzo steps aside and in a different voice says:)
	I'd really like to help. But what would people think? What would they say?
	(Lorenzo walks upstage and freezes.)
Narrator:	And now, meet Fagan Quagmire.
	(Fagan comes in and sees the injured person. Fagan also sees the other characters watching closely. Fagan goes to the injured person and says to the characters watching:)
Fagan:	What are you all doing? Why are you standing around?
Lorenzo:	Because it's cool, man!
Upton:	Can't cope, man!
Gerald:	Because he's a pretending whimp with no backbone!
Stanley:	Because everything is relative!
	(Fagan helps the injured person up. Fagan brushes the person off. Fagan takes his jacket off and gives it to the injured person. Fagan puts his arm around the injured person and looks at the others saying:)

Fagan:	Couldn't any of you have helped?

(The other characters turn away embarrassed. All the actors freeze. After a few moments' silence the narrator continues.)

Narrator:	Please stand for the Good News. The Lord be with you.
All:	And also with you.
Narrator:	A reading from the Good News according to Luke.
All:	Glory to you, Lord.

(Here the narrator or celebrant proclaims a passage from Luke's gospel: Lk. 10:25-37. At the conclusion of the passage, the narrator or celebrant says:)

Narrator:	And this is the gospel of the Lord.
All:	Praise to you, Lord Jesus Christ.

Finis

Theme:	Being our true selves.
Scripture:	Luke 10:25-37 *(The parable of the Good Samaritan)* or Colossians 3:12-17 *(Put on Christ)*
Props:	1. One animal headdress or disguise.
	2. Four masks on sticks — God, saint, angel and devil
	3. One pitchfork — cut out of sturdy cardboard.
	4. One stuffed hammer.
	5. One bonnet, shawl and purse for elderly Western woman.
	6. Two gun and holster sets.
	7. One white hat and black mask for the Lone Ranger.
	8. Two to six plastic silver bullets.
	9. One bandana and taxicab hat for burglar.
	10. One book for Stanley Noseinbook.
	11. One tattered shirt for Injured Person.

24

Production Notes: This dramatization was originally performed at a high school as part of a liturgical celebration near the feast of Halloween. Simplify or adapt the prop suggestions to your own situation and needs.

Study Questions:

1. Why do people wear masks, figuratively and literally? List and discuss some of the different masks that you have seen people wear.

2. Are there particular situations that occasion the wearing of masks more than others? What would some of these situations be?

3. What are some of the masks you wear? Do you use them to hide behind? What are you hiding? Why are you hiding?

4. When you fail to reveal what you are really thinking or feeling, aren't you putting on masks? Why do you do this? Do you have any alternatives?

5. What does it mean to put on Christ? How can this help you to reveal your true self? Is this easy? Is it important or worthwhile?

One Step Beyond

Cast:	Willingsford Pilgrim	Narrator
	Societal Pressure #1	Greed
	Societal Pressure #2	Gluttony
	Peer Pressure #1	Vanity #1
	Peer Pressure #2	Vanity #2
	Self-Doubt	Captain Freedom
	Self-Pressure	

Narrator: This is the story of one person's journey through the land of the living, encountering the dismal valley of distraction, on his way to that alluring place just beyond the horizon that is always annoyingly out of reach.

Meet Willingsford Pilgrim. Willy to his friends. Willingsford is about to begin a most fantastic journey through life to "The Freedom Zone," always just one step beyond.

As our story begins, we find the youthful Willingsford going where he wants to go, doing what he wants to do, having his way for the most part. Notice the serenity on Willy's face. Catch the hope and expectation gleaming through his eyes. Pay close attention to his winsome, unsuspecting smile. Don't overlook his unencumbered walk, those eager-for-adventure ears, that trusting nose. Watch him as he effortlessly makes his way along the Path of Life to Freedom.

Could our youthful hero suspect the danger that lies ahead? Could he possibly envision that his life is not a bowl of cherries? Could he sense the difficulties that lurk on this long road to freedom? Has he got the slightest inkling of an idea how many things will plague him, hound him, haunt him and taunt him, ultimately dragging him down and keeping him from his destination?

Well, as Willingsford unwittingly continues his journey through life, he encounters the first harbingers of disaster. He is set upon by those

27

hallucinous hobgoblins of the cosmos — Societal Pressures.

Societal-1: Hey, Willingsford, where are you going?

Societal-2: Yeah! Where you dancing off to? Taking your good old sweet time, aren't you?

Willy: I'm on my way, my merry old way, through life to a land of freedom.

Societal-1: Well, isn't that quaint!

Societal-2: You've got nothin' better to do than waste your time and ours on some fantastical journey to some fantastical place that only exists in your mind!

Societal-1: Who do you think you are?

Societal-2: Why don't you get a job?

Societal-1: Why don't you go to college?

Societal-2: When are you going to get married?

Societal-1: When are you going to settle down?

Societal-2: When?

Societal-1: When?

Societal 1 and 2: When?!!!

Narrator: Slowed slightly in his quest, swerved somewhat from his destination, Willy regains his composure and continues his journey. His gait is not as unencumbered. But still he continues. Little does our unsuspecting hero realize what lies ahead of him. If he was upset by those nasty societal pressures, he will be stunned by those ego mongols — Peer Pressure.

Peer-1: Hey, Willy boy, slow down, you're movin' too fast.

Peer-2: You've got to make the moment last.

Peer-1: You only go through life once, you know, so you've got to get all the gusto out of it that you can.

Peer-2: Yeah! You can't take it with you!

Peer-1: By the way, Billy boy, did you go out last night?

Peer-2: With a girl?

Peer-1: Did you have fun?

Peer-2: No, I mean did you really have fun? (*Willy doesn't understand.*)

Peer-1:	What's the matter, are you gay?
Narrator:	Pounded and battered by the pressure and penetration of their crazy querries, our pilgrim begins to show signs of fatigue on his journey. Will he be able to go on? Can it be that this is the end? Will he be able to muster the strength and courage to go on? Would you believe he will? Would you believe anything?
	And so our hero, weighed down by the torturous buffets of societal and peer pressure, slowly proceeds on his journey through life. Can he survive any more setbacks? Will he have a brief respite from grief? Are things looking up? Is this perhaps the dawning of a new day? Is there light shining at the end of the tunnel? Are clouds always darkest just before they break? There don't appear to be any obstacles outside of him. Perhaps he can do it now.
	But wait! Not so fast! Sure he's met and tangled with societal pressure and peer pressure, but he hasn't seen anything until he's locked in the death-dealing, strangulation grip of, you guessed it — Self-Doubt and Self-Pressure.
Self-Doubt:	Who do I think I'm fooling? I can't possibly do it! Nobody really likes me! Nobody cares whether I make it or not! I don't care if I make it or not! I don't care that I don't care! Nobody cares that I don't care that I don't care!
Self-Pressure:	And besides, everyone else is right! Why don't I study? Why don't I get married? Why don't I go to college? Why can't I settle down? Why can't I meet everybody's expectations? Why can't I meet my own expectations?
Narrator:	Our hero is stymied! He is paralyzed! Where is he to turn now? What is he to do? Is this the end? Not according to my script! Then what will he do for the next couple of pages? Why, go on! Sure he's bruised and beaten by the blows of self-doubt, societal and peer pressure, but who isn't? Willy Pilgrim will muster all the intestinal fortitude left in his distorted body and take that next sure step on his way along that winding, problem-riddled road to freedom. And as he does, who does he bump into but the blood and guts twins themselves — Greed and Gluttony.

Willy:	Hey fellows, give me a break. It's been a long day and I really want to be going.
Greed:	Sure you do. And we want to help you.
Gluttony:	Tired of the way things are? Want a change?
Greed:	Feel you're always being teased with a little bit of a good thing?
Gluttony:	Why there's nothing wrong with you that we can't fix.
Greed:	You're just blind to all that tantalizing good right under your nose.
Gluttony:	Why run off to someplace that might not even exist? Relax! A bird in the hand is worth two in the bush!
Greed:	Enjoy yourself! You need this and this and that. *(The Greed and Gluttony twins begin loading Willy down with different items.)*
Gluttony:	And this. And some more of this and that. Not to mention everything else. *(All these items can be simply covered sponge rubber or styrofoam. They can be put in Willy's shirt and pants to create a bloated effect.)*
Greed and Gluttony:	Munch, munch, chomp, chomp, with all of this you'll surely romp. *(Sung to Alka Seltzer tune.)*
	Slurp, slurp, drool, drool, grab everything and you'll be cool.
	Scarf, scarf, swallow, swallow, take all of this and you won't be hollow.
Narrator:	Is there no end to Willingsford's woes? Is this the what and when and why and wherefore of Willy's wasting away before our very eyes? Can he possibly go on weighed down as he is by so many pressures, so many cumbersome things?
	But wait! What is this? Is this the gameful Willy struggling even now to regain his balance and try again to reach the longed for land of freedom? Yes! It's true! He has begun again! Perhaps now he can scratch and claw his way to the end of the road. If only he does not have to face any further nuisances or obstacles.

	But alas, there are evil humors in the air. Clouds of unknowing point to more misery for our hapless hero. For just around the corner poor Willy is about to meet the last straw, the King and Queen of Serendipity — the Vanity Twins.
K-Vanity:	What have we here, sister?
Q-Vanity:	A pitiable pilgrim, brother? *(The two wear coats that open and reveal all sorts of products inside that include toothpaste, foot powder, certs, binaca, deodorant, shaving cream, spray paint, etc.)*
K-Vanity:	How can you stand going through life like this? You are totally unequipped!
Q-Vanity:	Do you like looking like this? Do you want to be like this forever?
K-Vanity:	Tired of having sand kicked in your face?
Q-Vanity:	Tired of being passed by, overlooked, stood up?
K-Vanity:	What's wrong with you, dude? You want to be in the groove? You're uncool!
Q-Vanity:	Here, try this! And some of this!
K-Vanity:	And this and this and this!
Q-Vanity:	And maybe just a squirt a day of this! *(Here Queen Vanity brings in a giant aerosal with "Body-All" written on it.)*
Narrator:	Well, friends, it looks like this is curtains for our pilgrim. There is simply no way he can go on this loaded down. Is this wee Willy's swan song? Is there nothing anyone can do? Is there no hope for our exhausted and humiliated pilgrim? Is this the end? Will Willy make it?
	But wait! Look! Up in the sky. Is it a duck-billed pladipus? No! Is it a blimp? No! Is it a flying bowling ball? Or an airborne frog? No! It's Captain Freedom!
Captain:	Here I am to save the day. Captain Freedom is on the way! Well, howdy pilgrim. Got some trouble here? Discovered it's a long road to freedom? A winding deep and wide? Feel that freedom's just another word for nothin's left to lose? Finding the freeway of life just a dirt beaten path? *(Lightning sound effect here).*
	Well, wake up, pilgrim! Captain Freedom's here to save the day! With my magical morsels you can

31

shake off all those shackles and be freedom bound.
With only one gulp of *(Lightning sound effect
again)* FREEDOM CRUNCHIES, kick those
devils out the door. Get those monkeys off your
back. New improved (Lightning sound effect
again) FREEDOM CRUNCHIES are fortified
with seven essential freedamins. They contain
beauty, power, social acceptance, strength and
success. They are fortified with multiple pat
answers. They'll enable you to win friends and
influence enemies. The extra additives of patience,
kindness and self-control will keep you from those
annoying highs and depressing lows. A special
extra vitamin BA for compliance with authority,
vitamin BS for making it through those myriad
social gatherings, and vitamin PH.D compound for
confirmation of your own self-worth.

So there, take it, pilgrim. Gulp them down!
Swallow them quickly and chase those blues away!
*(Captain hands Willy the box of Freedom
Crunchies.)*

Narrator: And there he goes, folks. Willy just swallowed
some of those Freedom Crunchies! Look at them
go to work immediately! Watch him blast through
societal pressures now! See him give peer pressure
what for! Look at him sock it to old self-doubt and
ego-pressure. Watch him bonk and zap old greed
and gluttony! And now look at him give the Vanity
twins the old one-two! That does it! He's free! He's
finally free of all those things that impeded his
progress! Look at him beam! Look at that smile of
satisfaction. Watch him take that easy,
unencumbered step to freedom now. Go on Willy,
we know you can do it now! *(Willy tries and falls
flat on his face.)*

Sorry Willy! Maybe it's not that easy. Maybe
freedom is somewhere out there, but just one step
beyond.

Finis

Theme: Freedom.

Scripture: John 8:32 *(The truth will set you free.)* or
2 Corinthians 3:17 *(Where the Spirit of the Lord is,
there is freedom.)*

Props:

1. Two stuffed instruments that are used by societal pressures as they interrogate Willy. They give him a blow with each question. Later self-doubt and self-pressure come in and give Willy these instruments and Willy hits himself at each of their questions.

2. Assorted items for the Greed and Gluttony twins. These can be spray painted pieces of foam rubber or styrofoam.

3. Assorted articles for the Vanity twins which can include: toothpaste, foot powder, certs, binaca, deodorant, shaving cream, spray paint, etc.

4. One gigantic aerosal can with "Body-All" written on it.

5. One Captain Freedom outfit. Use your imagination here.

6. One box of "FREEDOM CRUNCHIES".

7. One lightning sound effect recorded three times.

Production Notes:

Willingsford Pilgrim is given all sorts of acting suggestions through the narrative from the narrator. Use whatever suggestions the lines occasion. Remember to be sparing. You can never do everything.

This dramatization was originally done at a high school liturgy that was part of a series on the "Hungers of Humankind." The hunger treated in this celebration was that of freedom.

Study Questions:

1. What does freedom mean to you? Discuss the difference between "freedom from" and "freedom for."

2. What are the societal pressures Willy encounters? Do you experience anything similar in your own life? How do you deal with these questions that Willy must face as well as this type of pressure?

3. Can you think of any societal pressures Jesus experienced? How did he deal with them?

4. How do you experience peer pressure? What are some of the ways you deal with it? Can the phrase "To thine own self be true" give you any clues?

5. Was Jesus true to himself and others? Does being true to yourself mean dying sometimes? What are some of the things you must die to?

6. Was Jesus' life free of conflict? What are some Christian ways of dealing with that conflict?

7. What are the ways that you put pressure on yourself? What are the ways that you doubt yourself? Do the gospels give any clues as to how you can deal with these types of pressure? Share them.

8. How do greed and gluttony prevent us from being genuinely free? Discuss the ways you can be greedy or gluttonous in life.

9. What is wrong with Captain Freedom's Crunchies? Is there any easy way to become free? What must you do if you want to be free?

The Kingdom
That Was One

Cast:

Prince Shalom	Narrator
Escargot	Dog
Farmer	Toad
Baker	Rabbit
Butcher	Turtle
Barmaid	Bird
Cobbler	Cat
Minstrel	Fish
Jester	Town Crier
Candle Maker	

Narrator: Once upon a time, if you stretch your memory as far back as it can go, long before the time of penny candy and good five cent cigars, there existed the tiny kingdom of AT-ONE-MENT. And this was not your ordinary, every day, run of the mill kingdom. No, in the kingdom of AT-ONE-MENT, all the creatures lived together as one in peace and harmony.

The kingdom of AT-ONE-MENT was guided by the good Prince Shalom. *(The prince enters, riding an imaginary horse. There are outrageous applause and cheers by the inhabitants of the kindgom.)* He was wise and gentle, understanding and kind. All the people listened to him and he guided them wisely in the ways of all truth.

It is true that the inhabitants of AT-ONE-MENT were happy and united, but this did not happen over night. It had taken, and continued to demand, much time and effort on all of their parts to preserve this peace and unity unbroken. And what was their secret? Well, good Prince Shalom taught his people how to trust one another, how to accept their differences, and how to show their care by helping each other. Shalom had shown them how to look deeply into the eyes of every creature in the kingdom and see themselves.

Yes, Prince Shalom had taught his subjects to trust one another. Men, women, children and animals of all kinds were not suspicious of each other but walked and talked and worked and played together. Rabbits talked to people. People talked to fish. Fish talked to birds. And birds talked to... well, any and everyone who would listen to them.

Shalom also taught them to accept their differences. That some creatures walked and others flew, that some had shells and others tails, that some talked and others chirped, that some were pale and others dark, was not a cause for division, but only a source of glory and wonder and joy. For the desire of every creature's heart was to be at one with every other creature in the kingdom.

Toad: Can I help you?

Jester: Oh, thank you!

Rabbit: I don't know what we'll eat tonight!

Farmer: Well, I have more than enough vegetables. Here, take some of my carrots.

Baker: Yes, and some of my pastries!

Butcher: And some of my meat!

Narrator: Every creature in the kingdom of AT-ONE-MENT was unique. But together they were one in their trust, their desire and their care.

Now good Prince Shalom had an evil cousin who was a prince of darkness and a magician of the blackest arts. He was a scoundrel of the first order! He was mean! He was nasty! He was ugly! I mean, he really stunk! He sowed discord and perpetrated mischief wherever he went. He was a professor of the profane, a wizard of the worst, a grand master of deceit, and a prince of the putrid. His name was Escargot! *(The inhabitants of the kingdom boo and hiss. Escargot glares angrily at them.)*

Well, as our story continues, good Prince Shalom would have to leave the kingdom for long periods of time. *(As Prince Shalom rides away, the inhabitants wave and yell "goodbye." Escargot rides by Shalom into the kingdom. As Escargot passes Shalom, he waves and says "goodbye.")* Only this time, when Shalom left, evil Escargot snuck into the tiny kingdom of AT-ONE-MENT with the most horrible of intentions. He was set on sowing seeds of discord! He was determined to develop deadly divisions! He was resolved to create catastrophic carelessness and in general, foul up and demolish the unity and happiness of the tiny kingdom.

And so, Escargot embarked upon his evil work.

Escargot:	You, there, be careful about turning your back on people! You could get hurt!
Cat:	How? *(Escargot kicks the cat in the rump when the cat is not looking. The cat reacts and addresses the Barmaid.)* Now why did you do that?
Barmaid:	Do what?
Cat:	Why did you kick me?
Barmaid:	Don't be silly! I didn't kick you! *(Both the cat and the Barmaid turn away. Escargot kicks the cat again.)*
Cat:	Now don't tell me you didn't do it this time, you two-faced baboon!
Barmaid:	Oh, go pounce upon a mouse, you furry headed feline! *(Both the cat and the Barmaid freeze in their angry gestures.)*
Escargot:	Have you ever noticed what large ears those rabbits have?
Turtle:	Well, not really. But now that you mention it, they are kind of large!
Escargot:	Large? They're humongous! It's unnatural to have ears like that! Do you?
Turtle:	Why no! You're right! You know, I always did think that rabbit was a funny bunny! *(Rabbit comes towards Turtle unaware of what has been happening.)*
Rabbit:	Hi there, Telemachus Turtle!
Turtle:	Get away from me you, you, square hare! Tuck up your ears and scram!
Rabbit:	Buzz off yourself, you furless freak! Why don't you go sell your stinkin' shell! *(The turtle and the rabbit freeze.)*
Cobbler:	You horny toad!
Toad:	You flim-flam man!

Butcher:	You nurd bird!
Bird:	Killer!
All:	Weird! Weird! Odd! Odd! Different is truly ugly! *(They all freeze in a pointing gesture at each other.)*
Escargot:	Why help that dirty imperialistic dog? What did that dog ever do for you? You till the land, grow the crops and then the dog consumes them! What would happen if a drought came? You'd starve! Better he than thee! You're fooling yourself if you really think you ever have enough. When you help others, you only hurt yourself! Charity begins at home! So help yourself! Don't help! Hoard!
Minstrel:	You're right! Give me those vegetables!
Baker:	Give me those pastries!
Butcher:	And my meat!
All:	Gimme! Gimme! Gimme! Gimme! More! More! More! More! Gimme! Gimme! Gimme! Gimme! More! More! More! More! *(They all freeze in clutching gestures.)*
Narrator:	And so, evil Escargot, that dastardly deceiver, had succeeded in sowing seeds of division in the kingdom. And things went from bad to worse.
Town Crier:	Three o'clock and things are miserable! *(Crier breaks down into sobs.)*
Narrator:	Fear, distrust, cruelty, selfishness, dishonesty, all strangers in the little kingdom before, became the way of life. And all the inhabitants of the once united and happy kingdom were frustrated and very sad.
Jester:	Hey! Wait a minute! What kind of life is this? I thought that if we listened to you that we'd be really happy and content.
All:	Yeah! Yeah!
Escargot:	The reason it's not working is because you haven't taken that all important step. Stop looking into each others' eyes and seeing dreams of days gone by. Don't be attached to the past or dreams of anything! You've got to be careful. *(Escargot begins passing out sun glasses.)*

40

All:	We're carefree! We're carefree! We're happy! Happy and carefree!
Narrator:	Well, even though they protested that they were happy and carefree, they weren't! But at least they didn't have to see the hurt they caused when they read each other's faces and looked deeply into each other's eyes. They could hide behind the veil of tinted glass that evil Escargot had given them.
	And then one day good Prince Shalom returned to his kingdom and was astonished at what he saw.
Shalom:	I'm astonished!
Narrator:	Where once people trusted, now they only feared.
Candle:	After you.
Fish:	No! No! After you.
Candle:	I'm not as dumb as you look! After you!
Fish:	If you think that I'd turn my fin on you, you have another think coming!
Narrator:	Where once the inhabitants helped each other, now they only hoarded and hid. Anguished and dismayed, Shalom cried out to his people.
Shalom:	What has happened, my people? What is wrong?
All:	We're carefree! We're carefree!
Shalom:	Oh my friends, this is no way to be one or free! Gather around me! Open your ears and your hearts to what I have to say.
Narrator:	But evil Escargot, aware of the presence of his cousin once again in the kingdom, rushed in and tried to prevent the people from listening to Shalom's wise words. Escargot was determined to hold his evil power over them.
Escargot:	Get your handy-dandy ear plugs right here! His words will only cause you pain! Don't listen to him! Be happy! Be really carefree! Take my plugs and listen to me!
Jester:	Wait just a minute! You told us if we feared we'd be happy, and we weren't !
Turtle:	And if we hated one another's differences we'd be one, and we're not!
Butcher:	And if we helped ourselves first and foremost we'd be satisfied, and we aren't!

41

Rabbit:	And if we hid behind thoses glass veils we'd be truly happy and carefree, but it's not true! It's a lie! We have more worries than ever!
Shalom:	It's all lies, my friends. For Escargot is the Master of Deceit and Prince of Lies! Do you want to listen to me now?
All:	Yes!
Shalom:	Are you happy?
All:	No!
Shalom:	Would you like to change?
All:	Yes!
Shalom:	Would you like to be one again?
All:	Yes! With all our hearts we do!
Shalom:	Then first you must let go. You must not cling to anything. You must learn again how to share and help and care.
All:	But how?
Shalom:	Trust me, and I will show you! *(Here Shalom begins unclenching everyone's fists and arms. Gradually the animals and people begin helping each other.)*
	And now you must stop hiding behind those veils of tinted glass. You must take them off and look long and deeply into each other's eyes until you see yourself again in every creature.
All:	But we'll be blinded by the sun!
Shalom:	Just trust me and you will see, even if with great difficulty.
Narrator:	And good Prince Shalom was right. It was not an easy task for them to shed their comfortable veils. But slowly, surely, they helped each other remove the darkened glasses that had hidden the hurt they had worked on each other since evil Escargot had crept into the kingdom. Once the glasses were off they shielded their eyes. Then slowly, surely, they removed their hands from their faces. For the first time in a long, long time, they were looking into each other's eyes. They drew closer. They looked

	long and deeply. They saw in each other the anguish, hurt, frustration and sense of loss at what they once had. Then suddenly a tear began to creep into every creature's eyes and suddenly they could see their reflection again. Finally they were one again in the deepest desire of their hearts to forgive one another. *(Here all the people and creatures embrace.)*
Escargot:	Wait a minute, you sentimental sops! You bawling bumpkins! Stop! Stop! You fools! All, all fools! You haven't seen the last of me! It will take more than a quick hug to rebuild what I've undone! You think you can be one again? Well, it will cost you plenty! Maybe more than you are willing to give! And if that is the case, when you have tired of trying, I'll be there! Waiting! Ready! Poised and prepared to return! Until then, adieu you two legged and assorted furry fools! *(Escargot rides off on his imaginary horse.)*
Barmaid:	What shall we do?
Rabbit:	How can we keep him away from our kingdom?
Shalom:	Only if you are willing to spend much time and a lot of hard work will AT-ONE-MENT be free from the menacing evil of Escargot. Do you want to try again?
All:	Yes! Yes! A thousand times yes!
Shalom:	We have made a start! But it will take time for us to learn again, daily, how to trust one another, how to care for one another, how to be really one. But if we are all united in our heart's desire, I know we can do it this time. I know that in the end we can get it together! *(Here the whole cast sings the closing song.)*

Finis

Theme:	Reconciliation.
Scripture:	John 17:20-26 *(Let them all be one.)* or Luke 6:31-38 *(The measure you measure with will be measured back to you.)*
Props:	1. Four poles with castle-turret cut-outs attached.
	2. Four stands for the poles.
	3. One banner with the name AT-ONE-MENT written in bold letters on it.

43

4. One bell for the Town Crier.

5. A pair of sunglasses for each of the characters.

Production Notes: This dramatization was originally done at the Oakland Cathedral as part of a summer series on Reconciliation.

The different characters created simple costumes to indicate their profession or the type of animal they portrayed. Prince Shalom was dressed in white while Escargot wore black and a wizard's cap.

While three songs were sung by the cast in the original dramatization, this could easily be done without them. The music is included should you care to try it.

Once again the narration gives all sorts of clues as to the types of actions that can and should be performed by the different characters.

Study Questions: 1. Shalom taught the people of AT-ONE-MENT to accept their differences. Is this hard for you to do with others? Why or why not? What are things that could help you accept other's differences? Discuss.

2. How does Escargot divide the kingdom of AT-ONE-MENT? What tactics and arguments does he use? Have you ever felt this way towards others in your life? Why?

3. What do the sun glasses symbolize? Discuss the different ways you can be blind and oblivious to the hurt you may inflict on others? What can you do in order to become more sensitive and aware?

4. What did Prince Shalom have to do in order to bring his kingdom back together again? What were the steps? What would you have to do in order to live with others? Discuss.

5. Discuss the differences between carefree and careful.

6. What does Prince Shalom symbolize? What does Escargot symbolize? How can you keep Escargot away from your families and communities? Discuss.

7. Is reconciliation easy? Is it important? Does it play a regular or important part in your life? How can it? Discuss.

8. Rollo May, in his book *The Courage To Create*, says that contemporary people need the courage to be (1) vulnerable, (2) intimate, and (3) committed. How would these three courages help you to be a reconciled and reconciling community? Discuss.

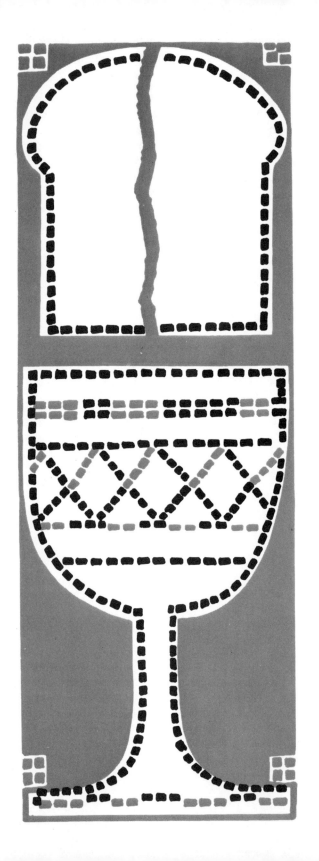

The Tale Of The Town With The Strange Forgotten Name

Cast:	Narrator	
	Charlotten B. Pomposity (Mayor)	Citizen-1
	Thorton U. Pinchpenny (Banker)	Citizen-2
	Little Nelly Alswell	Citizen-3
	Purdy Quagmire (Grandpa)	Citizen-4
	Justin Dogood	Placard Bearer
	Panis Angelicus (Baker)	
	I. Cantrell Dumond (Black Bart)	

Scene One:

Narrator: Back in the days of buckskin, boarding houses and brave handsome beaus, back when the West was wild and full of adventure, back in the year 1876, the first centennial of this proud nation......

Citizen-3: *(Singing)* I'm a Yankee Doodle Dandy, Yankee Doodle do or die...

Grandpa: I sure am glad these celebrations only come once every hundred years.

Narrator: Well, way back when the West was young, there was a little town nestled in the Nevada desert where all the inhabitants lived together happily in peace. They were all concerned for one another and took care of every person's needs. Except for their constant care for one another, it would have been a town of "Haves" and "Have Nots." As it was, those who were in need were helped by those who had much. No one ever went without. The people helped one another and shared all they had together: the good things, the hard things, their joys and sorrows. The leader of this happy hamlet was the less than honorable Charlotten B. Pomposity.

Citizen-1: We sure are proud of you, Mr. Pomposity.

Mayor: That's Pomposity, you bumbling bumpkin!

Narrator:	The wealthiest and second most influential person in town was Thornton U. Pinchpenny, president of the Bank D'Argent.
All:	D'Argent?
Banker:	That's French for money. But the people around here just refer to it as the B of A.
Narrator:	The prettiest girl in town, a flower of untainted virtue and goodness, a petal unstained by the evil of this world, a blossom of such incomparable innocence....
Nelly:	Aaahemmmmm!
Narrator:	Excuse me. I did get a bit carried away. As I was saying, the prettiest girl in town was Little Nelly Alswell. She lived with her grandfather, Purdy Quagmire.
All:	Grandfather?
Narrator:	Well, on her mother's side, of course!
All:	Oh!
Nelly:	Oh Grandpa *(Nelly pats Purdy on the back. Purdy's back has been generously covered wth flour or baby powder so that whenever anyone pats him on the back a cloud of dust arises.)*, isn't it a truly blessed existence to live in Shareiswhereitsat?
Purdy:	I guess so, but I sure will never understand the name of this darn ole town.
Narrator:	Also living in Shareiswhereitsat were Nel's beau or boyfriend, Justin Dogood, and a baker, a man most people considered to be the wisest, kindest man in town, Mr. Panis Angelicus.
Baker:	Would you like some of my freshly baked bread?
Citizen-4:	Yes sir, I would. But I ain't got no money.
Baker:	Well, that's alright.
Citizen-4:	But how can I repay you?
Baker:	By giving from your abundance one day when someone else is in need.
Narrator:	Everything was peaceful and serene in Shareiswhereitsat. But would things remain this way? Are there storm clouds on the horizon? Could anything or anyone destroy the goodness and serenity of this little town?

Narrator:	Into this serene setting, one day, came I. Cantrell Dumond, President of the Blatantly Avaricious Railway Transport Company, vulgarly referred to as B.A.R.T. *(Placard with "BOO" is raised.)*
Bart:	*(He snickers at the hisses and boos.)* How do you do? My name is I. Cantrell Dumond. *(Placard with "BOO" is raised.)*
Mayor:	What do your friends call you?
Bart:	Bart!
Banker:	And what do your enemies call you?
Bart:	Black Bart! *(Placard with "HISS" is raised.)*
Narrator:	And so, Black Bart slipped into town one day. You might be asking yourselves what a dastardly, sinister, no-good, low-down, nasty, despicable, diabolical person like Black Bart was doing in Shareiswhereitsat?
Citizen-2:	Yeah! What is he doing here?
Narrator:	I'm glad you asked that question. You see, unbeknownst to the townspeople, Black Bart *(He says "Ha! Ha!")* was in cohoots with the mayor Charlotten B. Pomposity *(He says "Ho! Ho!")* and the bank president Thorton U. Pinchpenny *(He says "Hee! Hee!")*. Together they would stop at nothing in order to get the railroad to run through Shareiswhereitsat. *(Placard with "BOO" is raised.)* The townspeople loved Shareiswhereitsat. They neither needed nor wanted the railroad. This meant that the only way Black Bart could get his way was to destroy the town or make the people so miserable that they would want to move away.
Bart:	Now let's get down to business.
Mayor:	Yeah! How are we gonna drive them outta this town? The dang fools like it here in the desert!
Bart:	Listen, idiots, they like it here because they're satisfied with what they've got. We have to get them to want something else!
Banker:	What's that?

Bart:	What's that?!! Why you ironed-brain fool! Don't you see? What is it that you really crave? That your mouth waters for? That your whole being hungers for?
Mayor:	An ice cream soda?
Bart:	Oh shut up! More than an ice cream soda! More than your Teddy Bear! More than a hug from dear ole Mom!
Banker:	Money?
Bart:	Yes! What do you love the cold, hard feel of? *(The Banker responds to each of Bart's questions with the word "money" spoken louder and louder each time.)* The clinking sound of? The lovely green look of? Yes! Yes! And what is it that's no good unless you have more of it than somebody else? And what is it that people will cheat for? And steal for? And kidnap each other's teddy bears for? And sell their mothers for?
Banker:	Money! Money! Money! Oh, I'll take care of this. It's right up my alley! I'll make them so greedy that they'll destroy each other fighting for money and goods!
Bart:	And when you're done, you'll own the whole town! *(Placard with "BOO" is raised.)*
Banker:	Yes, I'll be rich! rich! rich!
Mayor:	But what about me?
Bart:	You, my good man? Why you're the Mayor, and that is your secret weapon. Because you know what people want even more than money!
Mayor:	I do?
Bart:	Of course you do! What do people use their money for?
Mayor:	Big Macs?
Bart:	No idiot! For honor! Honor: the food of the soul!
Mayor:	Honor?
Bart:	Of course! What is the sustenance of a person's spirit? *(The Mayor responds to each of Bart's questions with the word "honor" spoken louder and louder each time.)* The nourishment that makes a person great? And what is money useless without?

Mayor:	Honor!
Bart:	And what do people always want from one another?
Mayor:	Honor!
Bart:	And what will people die to defend?
Mayor:	Their honor! Oh, I'll be famous! I'll be great! After we take over this town, I'll become a State Senator, then Governor, then United States Senator, then, then...
Narrator:	Could the unsuspecting townspeople comprehend the evil that lurks in these devils' hearts? Would they simply be pounced upon? Would evil have its day? *(Placard with "horrors" is raised.)*

Scene Three:

Narrator:	And so this serpentine trio set about their dirty tricks campaign. First, Thornton U. Pinchpenny worked his poison.
Banker:	You never know when a famine will fall upon you and hard times set in. You never know when there will be a shortage of anything. Why share your money and goods when you might need them some day? *(To Citizen-2)* Besides, he's found oil on his property and hasn't told anyone else about it. See? He's no dummy! Wise up, you prodigal peasant! Greed's the seed that solves your need!
Citizen-1:	Could you loan me a cup of sugar?
Citizen-2:	Certainly, if you loan me a cup of oil!
Citizen-1:	But I don't have a cup of oil!
Citizen-2:	Then I don't have a cup of sugar. So scram!
Narrator:	Now instead of sharing all they had, the townspeople hoarded.
Baker:	There's something rotten in the state of Nevada.
Narrator:	Next, Charlotten B. Pomposity sowed new seeds of discontent. *(Citizen-3 and Citizen-4 bump into each other.)*
Citizen-3:	Excuse me.
Citizen-4:	O certainly!
Mayor:	You grovelling gutless whelp! Are you going to let him get away with that?

Citizen-4:	But he didn't mean to.
Mayor:	O yes he did, you grungy pea-brained urchin! Have you no honor? A person will shrivel up and die without honor! Honor is food for your soul! Who needs apologies? Be strong! It's the meek who are weak, you backboneless milk-sop! *(Citizen-3 and Citizen-4 bump into each other again.)*
Citizen-3:	Excuse me.
Citizen-4:	Beat it, you creep!
Citizen-3:	Go to! Go to! you pugnacious punk!
Narrator:	Soon all the people of Shareiswhereitsat were at odds with each other. *(The townspeople turn their backs on one another.)*
Baker:	When will the people come to their senses? How long must they continue to hurt each other?
Narrator:	Finally, Black Bart himself worked his worst deceit.
Bart:	These two fools! Did they really think I would share all of this with them? Now I will set them and the whole town against each other. *(To the Banker)* Do you know what the Mayor is doing? He is organizing the Have-nots to march against you and the Haves.
Banker:	Whatever will I do?
Bart:	Well, you better get off your duff and do something. *(The Banker begins to organize the Haves. While this is going on, Bart speaks to the Mayor.)* Do you know what Thornton U. Pinchpenny is doing? He's organizing the Haves to march against you and the Have-nots.
Mayor:	Alas! What should I do?
Bart:	Organize! Strike! Fight! Beat them to the punch!
Narrator:	And so, the town was split into two camps. The once serene town was filled with unhappiness. Could anyone do anything to remedy this horrendous situation? Was there any way out of this perplexing predicament? Where is that baker? Who is Panis Angelicus?

Narrator:	The townspeople were very unhappy. Finally, one day, little Nel confided to her Grandpa.
Nelly:	O Grandpa, I am so miserable! Everyone is so unhappy! Why are things so rotten, so foul, so askew?
Grandpa:	Gazunteit!
Nelly:	O Grandpa, I was not sneezing. What should I do?
Grandpa:	The only one who can help us now is Mr. Panis Angelicus. Why not go and ask him what we should do.
Narrator:	And so, Nel made her way to Panis Angelicus' bakery. Once there she bared her soul to Mr. Panis Angelicus.
Nelly:	Oh, Mr. Panis Angelicus, what has happened to our once serene and wonderful little town? Why are things so rotten, so foul, so askew?
Baker:	Gazunteit!
Nelly:	Oh, Mr. Angelicus, I wasn't sneezing. What can we do?
Baker:	Little Nel, the town is unhappy because the people have forgotten how to share, to give, to forgive! People have forgotten how to put the needs of others before their own. They are afraid! They are starved for love and yet will not avail themselves of the medicine that can cure them.
Nelly:	Which is?
Baker:	Which is beginning again and learning how to share with each other; learning how to give and forgive; learning how to die to selves and live for others. All those things that once made this town so great!
Nelly:	O, Mr. Angelicus, we had all forgotten. I must run now and remind all the people. Perhaps it is not too late and they will listen!
Narrator:	But little did Little Nel and Mr. Angelicus realize that Black Bart had overheard their entire conversation. Bart knew that this would completely thwart his plans. And so, this venomous viper decided to kidnap Little Nel *(Placard with "HISS" is raised.)* and ride to the

	high country, there to explode the dam and destroy the entire town. *(Placard with "HORRORS" is raised.)* And so, Black Bart grabbed Little Nel. She screamed!
Nelly:	Help! Help! Save me! Save me!
Justin:	Never fear, Justin's here!
Bart:	Curses, foiled again! But not for long.
Narrator:	And with that, Black Bart gave Justin Dogood a mighty right uppercut to his Promethean jaw that stuck out and almost invited attack. And so Black Bart galloped away towards the dam and destruction. Suddenly Justin came to. Mr. Panis Angelicus ran out.
Baker:	Justin Dogood, what has happened?
Justin:	O Mr. Panis Angelicus, Black Bart has dealt a foul blow to my chin and ridden off with Little Nel. What does this mean?
Baker:	It means he overheard us! Come, quickly gather the people!
Narrator:	And so the people gathered quickly. *(The townspeople rush in from different places.)*
All:	What has happened? What has happened? Tell us! Tell us!
Baker:	My people, you are all unhappy because of the work of Black Bart and the help of our Mayor and Bank President. *(These two look embarrassed.)* You have forgotten how to share. Instead you have been greedy, proud and desirous of power to dominate instead of to serve. This must stop now before it is too late! Even now Black Bart has kidnapped Little Nel and ridden off to destroy the dam. We must set aside our differences and once again work together. To the dam!
Narrator:	And so the people united and pursued. Was it too late? Was Little Nel doomed? Could the people find their serenity again riding off to a dam? Why didn't Grandpa ride off with them? What will happen to Mr. Panis Angelicus?

Scene Five:

Narrator:	There followed a chase of Cecil B. Demillish proportions. *(Here there is a choreographed chase scene accompanied by "chase" music.)* Finally Black

54

Bart arrived at the dam and set the charges to go off. Justin Dogood and the townspeople were right behind them. I said Justin Dogood and the townspeople were right behind them. When they reached the dam, Justin ran across the top of the dam to rescue Little Nel. He struggled with Black Bart. *(All the townspeople shout "STRUGGLE! STRUGGLE! STRUGGLE!")* but this time it was Bart who fell. *(The placards with "APPLAUSE" and "CHEERS" are raised.)* Justin swept Little Nel up and ran to the safety of the mountains. There were cheers of joy *(The townspeople cheer.)* that good had triumphed. But the cheers were suddenly turned to horror when they all heard an explosion of gigantic proportions. *(First there is the sound effect of an explosion. Then the placard with "HORRORS" is raised.)* The charges had gone off after all. The dam broke and the town was lost.

Nelly: Now what will we do?

Citizen-1: All is lost!

Citizen-2: Our homes!

Citizen-3: Our families and friends!

Citizen-4: All our hopes washed away.

Nelly: But what is this? My dear Grandpa coming towards us puffing up the hill!

Narrator: Nel was right. Purdy Quagmire had not perished in the flood.

Nelly: Grandpa, how did you escape?

Grandpa: Folks, everything is alright. Mr. Panis Angelicus and I stayed behind and helped evacuate all the old, young, lame and infirm townspeople just in case the dam broke.

Justin: Where is this gallant, wise and gracious man so we can thank him?

Grandpa: Unfortunately, as he had gotten the last person to safety, he himself was swallowed by the flood of water. He is gone. *(All heads fall sadly.)*

Nelly: What shall we do now? All is lost!

Justin: O no it's not! Mr. Panis Angelicus brought us to our senses. He has taught us something. We can begin again. Now finally our eyes are open and we can see.

Grandpa:	Yeah! And maybe we can get a new name for our town. I never did understand the old one.
Nelly:	Neither did I until today, Grandpa. It's not Shareiswhereitsat, it's Share-Is-Where-It's-At.
Mayor:	I have learned my lesson.
Banker:	And so have I.
All:	So have we all!
Justin:	Thanks to Mr. Panis Angelicus. Let us always remember what has happened here, and what we have learned, by gathering together often and sharing the bread Mr. Angelicus himself made and gave to us. As we break the bread, let our eyes be open so we can see that it is in giving that we receive, it is in forgiving others that we experience forgiveness, and it is in dying each day that we are born to true life. *(The placard with "APPLAUSE" is raised.)*

Finis

Theme:	The Hungers of the World
Scripture:	John 6:35-51 *(The Bread of life discourse)* or Luke 24:13-35 *(The Disciples of Emmaus)*
Props:	1. Five large placards — each placard should have one of the following words printed on it in large, bold letters: BOO, HISS, HORRORS, APPLAUSE, CHEERS.
	2. Assorted whistles — if they are available you may use some sound effects to liven up the production. We used a train whistle for reference to the railroad, a siren whistle for hustling and bustling situations and a slide whistle for assistance in communicating moods of moving from joy to sorrow or vice versa.
	3. Assorted costumes — whatever you can piece together. In the original production of this story dramatization we used the following costuming. Black Bart was in white shirt, black shoes, socks, pants, vest, tail coat and cape with a black stove pipe hat. He wore a black handlebar mustache. The Mayor wore a three piece suit with a sash from his left shoulder to right side of his waist. The Banker wore a vest and visor. Little Nel wore a long dress, a bonnet and pigtails. Justin Dogood wore a

cowboy outfit. Panis Angelicus wore a white apron and white chef's hat. The townspeople wore assorted garb.

4. Sound effects — besides the whistles, it would be effective to have a recorded sound effect of an explosion. Other helpful musical suggestions will be made in the production notes.

Production Notes: This story dramatization was originally performed at the Oakland Cathedral during their Bicentennial summer liturgy series. The series dealt with the hungers of the world. This particular dramatization focused on Jesus Christ as the food that satisfies.

Since this story drama is cast in the genre of Melodrama, it should be played broadly. Actions and reactions should be exaggerated and stylized.

A piano player who can play a few bars of theme music for the major characters when they appear, as well as some appropriate chase and mood music will add tremendously to the flow of the dramatization as well as impact.

Every time the crowd boos or hisses Black Bart, he should scowl at them and raise a clenched fist.

If a eucharist or communion service follows the proclamation of the Word, have Mr. Panis Angelicus bring up the bread.

Study Questions: 1. Try and think of as many things as you can that people hunger for. Don't just limit yourself to food. What are some of the things you hunger for? What about affection, acceptance and approval for starters? Discuss these and explore others.

2. Who is Panis Angelicus? Does he remind you of any other characters living or dead? Why was he considered so gentle, caring and wise?

3. What did Panis Angelicus teach the townspeople by his example? Talk about the people who have most influenced you by what they said and did. What did you learn from them? Is that important? Why or why not?

4. What do you think of Black Bart's description of money? Do you agree or disagree? Why? How important is money in your life? Explore the ways

that money can be helpful to you. When would it not be helpful? Why? Discuss.

5. What do you think of Black Bart's description of honor? Do you agree or disagree? How important is honor and the opinion of others in your life? When is this helpful and when can it become dangerous? Discuss.

6. Does the story drama give any clues as to how we can avoid a world of "haves" and "have-nots?" What would this entail? Would it be easy? Compare this to the situation of the early Christians as described in the Acts of the Apostles, either chapter two verses forty-two to forty-seven or chapter four verses thirty-two to thirty-five.

7. How are we as Christians called to start over again and again? How is forgiveness related to this? What are the places in your life and in our world where you would like to make some new beginnings? How could you go about this? Discuss and explore.

8. How can we become more aware of World Hunger today? How can we creatively work to share more of our natural resources with those who have little or nothing? How many organizations in your city or state or country have information or programs related to World Hunger? Try and investigate these and their programs by obtaining and studying their literature.

Witterhans

Cast:	Narrator	Citizen-1
	Hans Pilgrim	Citizen-2
	E. Manuel Dexterity	Citizen-3

Narrator: Once upon a time, in a land very much like our own earthen sod, there was a town called Witterhans. Witterhans was not like other towns. For all the inhabitants had lost the use of their hands. It wasn't that they didn't have hands, somehow they had forgotten how to use them. And this presented many difficulties to the timid little inhabitants of Witterhans.

All those townspeople who wore hats couldn't tip them to their neighbors as they strolled down the street. Because when they bowed their heads, their hats would fall off. And there was simply no way that they could pick them up and put them back on. But they certainly looked funny when they tried.

The inhabitants of Witterhans couldn't wave hello or goodbye. They couldn't wave to get someone's attention. There was no clapping of hands in appreciation of all the good things they saw and heard. They could only stamp their feet. And whenever they did this, it always sounded like charging rhinos or a herd of angry buffaloes.

No one could knock on a door to announce their arrival. They could only bump their heads against them which was very painful and confusing to all who lived within. Of course, they couldn't use their hands to eat or drink, and so food and liquids made their faces humongously messy. They became icky-sticky-gooey-foooey!

No one in the town could write a letter and you know how awkward it can be to write with your toes or hold a pen in your mouth. They couldn't comb their hair or wash their faces or dry them once they had dipped them in water, so there was naturally a lot of dandruff and scaley skin in Witterhans.

Hitchhiking had long ago been outlawed because nobody could "thumb a ride." But what was most inconvenient was that no one could scratch their itches. They had to imitate the bears and rub up against trees and sharp objects and hope they didn't hurt themselves. Most games were out of the question for the Witterhansites. They couldn't play basketball or baseball or tennis or racketball, but they were excellent soccer players.

The young people of Witterhans had all sorts of trouble in school. They couldn't read very easily since they had to turn the pages with their noses. And they didn't learn very much because nobody could raise their hand to ask a question.

The church of Witterhans was in dire financial straits because no one could take up a collection. The Town Council went nowhere because they could never arrive at decisions. Decisions meant voting and voting required, you guessed it, a show of hands.

There was no art, no music, no painting, no culture. The people of Witterhans led a pretty dull life. Promises were never made because nobody could "shake on it." And oaths were never heard because no one could raise their right or left hand.

But worst of all, children couldn't hold hands and run and jump and play. No inhabitant could offer a "helping hand" to townspeople in need. And this made them all very sad. It hurt, too, never being able to express care or love with the gentle touch of a hand.

The inhabitants were frustrated day and night. Theirs was a sad, sad lot. Finally, one day, one of the inhabitants of Witterhans said to himself:

Hans: Self, I've had it! There has got to be a better way. This whole frustrating predicament is getting out of hand. If I don't get away from here, I'm going to fly off the handle. I have to find some help.

Narrator: This was Hans Pilgrim, a young member of the town. And so Hans struck out on his own to see if he could find relief for himself and all his friends in the town of Witterhans. He walked many miles for many days and nights. Then one day, as Hans was walking along kicking every other loose stone in the road, he happened upon a most remarkable man named E. Manuel Dexterity. "Manny" to his friends. As they passed, E. Manuel noticed Hans and hailed him.

Manny: Ohhhhh! How do you do? My name is E. Manuel Dexterity, but you will never remember that. Just call me Manny, for short. Put it there, pal! *(Manny sticks out his right hand to shake but Hans only offers him his shoulder.)* Ohhhh! Giving me the cold shoulder, ehhh? Or is that your warm one? Ha! Ha! Ha! Isn't that a knee slapper? *(Here Manny slaps his raised knee. Hans tries to imitate him but can only raise his knee.)* Tell me, friend, what's your name?

Hans: Hans Pilgrim, sir, from the town of Witterhans.

Manny: What a delightfully unusual name. Well now, Hans, can you point the way to Witterhans? *(Hans nods his head.)* Now what do we have here, a nervous twitch? Don't you get the gist of my request? I need directions? Can't you point? What's your problem, child?

Hans: My problem is that I get the point. But the point is that I can't point!

Manny: What?!!?

Hans: I mean that I can't point with my hands. As a matter of fact, I can't do anything with my hands.

Manny: Ohhhh! Likkkkeeee, yesssssss. I see. Well, of course that's simply dreadful!!! Hands! Hands! Can't use your hands! I've always been able to use my hands! Ever since I learned! *(Manny throws his cane at Hans who instinctively catches it. To do this he brings his hands out of his pockets.)* Now the strange thing about hands is that they are absolutely no good to you unless you use them! *(Here Manny throws his hat to Hans who catches it.)* I remember a man once who wouldn't use his hands for twenty years or so. I mean that he wouldn't use them for anything but hoarding. He gathered, gathered, gathered! He never gave a single thing away. He used his hands solely for holding on to everything he possessed. His friends called him Grabby Hayes. Old Grabby was afraid of losing anything he had so he finally put his hands and all he had into his pockets and left them there. Grabby's family never knew how to do anything with their hands either except to stick them tight-fisted into their pockets. *(Manny throws his gloves to Hans who catches them.)* Such a pity, too. Just think of all the wonderful things he could have done with them. Now just why can't you use your hands?

Hans: Because they're in my.......*(Suddenly Hans realizes that his hands are out of his pockets.)* I don't believe it! My hands! I can see them! I can feel them!

Manny: And you can use them, pilgrim! Now what simply marvelous hands you have! Just think of all the things you can do with them now. *(Hans taps his fingers on his head imagining. Then he throws his hands up in joy. He could even act out a few of the things he can do with them.)* You simply must use them now. It would be such a shame to waste them now that you've found them.

Hans: I can't believe this! I can really use my hands. Do you think you could possibly come and show my friends how to use their hands?

Manny: No! No! No time! No time! I must keep going! Miles to go before I sleep! All sorts of things to do! Besides, you can show them. The old principle, you know, "pass it on and don't return it!" You must do it! You must do it!

Hans: But how?

Manny: Just remember how I taught you. Just try. Discover. Share with your friends all that you have learned and much more. So sorry, now, I must be going! T.T.F.N.!

Hans: Huh?

Manny: You know, Ta Ta For Now!

Hans: May I keep these things?

Manny: You may have the hat and gloves, but the cane stays with me! Adieu!

Narrator: And so, Hans Pilgrim returned in joy to Witterhans. He was happy in his newly recovered gifts and was determined to share his good fortune! The inhabitants of the town were amazed. They could hardly believe their eyes. They tried to rub them in disbelief, but forgot that they still didn't

	know how to use their own hands. Finally they asked him.
Citizen-1:	Hans, what in the world has happened to you?
Citizen-2:	How in God's green earth did you ever learn to use your hands?
Hans:	I met the most remarkable person. He showed me how to use my hands. He opened up to me all the fantastic things you can do with them.
Citizen-3:	But how did he do that?
Hans:	Actually it's quite simple! *(Hans throws a glove at Citizen-3 who instinctively takes his/her hands out of pockets and catches it.)* You really don't have to think about it for very long. No reason to get a mental hernia over it! *(Hans throws the other glove at Citizen-2 who also reflexively brings his/her hands out and catches it.)*
Citizen-1:	He must have used some pretty strong magic.
Hans:	On the contrary, no magic involved at all! All you have to do is use the hands you have and could have used all along if you had only known that you could use them! *(Hans throws the hat to Citizen-1 who also brings his/her hands out to catch it.)* Now why can't you all use your hands?
All:	Because we have them in our......*(They realize that their hands are no longer in their pockets.)* We can use our hands!
Narrator:	And, oh, what joy there was in Witterhans that day, my friends. For the first time the inhabitants could express their joy with their newly rediscovered gift. It took much time, but the townspeople patiently and gradually learned to do so many wonderful things now that they had their hands back.
	They could tip their hats. They could greet each other with waves of welcome and farewell. The sound of charging rhinos was transformed into the thunder of appreciative applause. They could write one another. They gradually learned not only how to tithe with their hands in church, but to pray with them as well.
	They could offer gifts and share with their hands. They could bless one another and exchange signs of friendship. Things were finally decided at town hall

65

meetings. Witterhans became famous for their tremendous ability to "lend a helping hand" to all in need. They learned to touch everything and everyone with gentleness and care.

All the people explored and discovered how they could think with their hands, and feel with their hands, and express with their hands, and give with their hands. And when they played in the wet grass for too long, they could use their hands to get at those elusive itches.

For the rest of their lives they continued to explore and share with those they met the joy of rediscovering the gift of their hands.

Finis

Theme: The Gifts in our Lives.

Scripture: I Corinthians 12:4-11 *(Variety of Gifts but always the same Spirit)* or
2 Corinthians 8:1-15 *(A question of balancing)*

Props: 1. One pair of gloves.

2. One hat.

3. One cane.

4. Costuming — according to taste and means. E. Manuel Dexterity should be nattily dressed. The townspeople can be simply dressed.

Production Notes: This dramatization was originally performed in a liturgy at Holy Names College in Oakland, California. It was on the occasion of the first official Sunday that Catholics in the United States could receive communion in the hand. It was because of this that I wished to stress that we were not receiving a new gift but simply rediscovering and reclaiming an old one.

If this dramatization is used in a worship service, it would be an excellent opportunity to invite the community to use their hands in different ways *(i.e., confessing, praying, receiving, caring, blessing, etc.)*

Study Questions: 1. Why can't the people of Witterhans use their hands? What caused them to forget? What do they have to do in order to be able to use their hands again?

66

2. Think of all the different ways you can use your hands. Discuss. What are some of the feelings you can communicate with your hands? Explore. What are some of the ways you can use your hands in worship? Explore.

3. Are there people like E. Manuel Dexterity who have come into your life and revealed to you your giftedness in ways you hadn't experienced before? Discuss and share. How did they do this for you?

4. Spend some time reflecting on what some of your personal gifts are. Share your reflections with the group.

5. Have each member of your group become the individual focus for the whole group. Have members of the group reflect on the giftedness of this person. What are some of the gifts that the group sees in you that you may have been blinded to? What makes it difficult for you to look on these aspects of who you are as gift? Explore.

6. St. Paul reflects on the gifts of the Christian community in the twelfth chapter of the first letter to the Corinthians. Read about these and then reflect on what the contemporary gifts of your church or class are. What are the gifts your family or class or church need at this time? Is it alright if we all don't have the same gifts? How can we learn to appreciate the gifts of others? Explore and discuss.

7. Do you experience yourself as a gift? Why or why not? How can you express gratitude for the gift of self? Is it easy or hard for you to share yourself with others? Brainstorm and share some of the creative ways to share more of yourself with others.

8. What is a paradox? Do you experience any paradoxes in your life? Discuss. What is a Christian paradox? In the concluding part of the Prayer of St. Francis we pray: "For it is in giving that we receive, it is in pardoning others that we ourselves are pardoned, and it is in dying that we are raised to life." Is this sense or nonsense for a Christian? How can we, as Christians, live out the words of this prayer? Explore and discuss.

Prophet-Sharing School

Cast:	**Otto Von Stoop** **Beatrice Urself** **Gert Bonk** **Mime** **Rosie Daifter** **Reader**

Otto: *(He moves to the podium or microphone as do the other teachers and the mime. They all sing with him:)* This is the way we go to school, go to school, go to school. This is the way we go to school to learn to be a prophet. They're all in their places with bright shining faces. Good morning class.

All: *(The mime holds up a placard that says:)* Good morning, Professor.

Otto: Welcome to our first annual summer-school of prophet-sharing. You look like an excellent group of candidates and we are glad you could come. Aren't we, professors?

Professors: Yes, we are very glad you could come.

Otto: Now some of you are asking yourselves or your neighbors, "Who is this cock-a-doodle-doo?" Aren't you?

All: *(The mime holds up a placard that says:)* Right!

Otto: Well, my name is Baron Otto Von Stoop. I am Headmaster of the J. C. Emmanuel Prophet-Sharing School. And let me introduce you to my staff. *(Otto holds up his walking stick.)* I would also like you to meet the professors who will be instructing you. First, the Professor of Criticism, Gert Bonk. Next, the Professor of Energy, Ms. Rosie Daifter. Thirdly, our Professor of Uniquity, Ms. Beatrice Urself. And assisting the professors will be our Instructor of Symbolic Action, *(mime's name)*. So, now I call school to order. Are you ready to begin?

All: *(The mime holds up a placard that says:)* No.!

Otto: Well, what's the matter?

Reader:	(*A man or a woman with a good speaking voice will be the first reader. They are planted in the congregation.*) We aren't prophets, professor. We are just ordinary men, women and children. Some of us are mothers, some fathers, some students, business people or workers. We aren't prophets.
Otto:	Not now, maybe, but you will be when we get through with you. (*Musing to himself.*) You know, you sound just like a graduate of our school from many years ago in another time and another place. His name was Amos. Would you help me share with the people a little story about Amos?
Reader:	How?
Otto:	Come here. (*Otto gets the Book of Scriptures.*) Receive the Word of God and share it with your brothers and sisters. After all, that is what a prophet is called to do.
Reader:	But I couldn't... I... I...
Otto:	Go on. Go on. You can do it. Try!
Reader:	(*The reader timidly approaches the microphone and begins.*)

A reading from the book of the prophet Amos. (*Am. 7:12-15.*) Amaziah (*priest of Bethel*) said to Amos, "Off with you, visionary, flee to the land of Judah! There earn your bread by prophesying, but never again prophesy in Bethel; for it is the king's sanctuary and a royal temple." Amos answered Amaziah, "I was no prophet, nor have I belonged to a company of prophets; I was a shepherd and a dresser of sycamores. The Lord took me from following the flock, and said to me, 'Go, prophesy to my people Israel.' "

This is the Word of the Lord.

(*Then the reader returns to his/her seat.*)

Otto:	Very good. Very good. You see, Amos was just an ordinary person minding his own business like you. But like Amos, each of us is called as a Christian to be prophetic by all we say and all we do. So onwards and upwards.

Now first we must matriculate you into our school. So, we give you an entrance exam to see who qualifies for entrance into our school. If you can answer "I am" or "yes" to any of the following questions, just stand. All those who stand, qualify.

How many of you are called to be loving fathers?
How many of you are called to be loving mothers?
How many of you are called to be loving children?
How many of you are called to be loving brothers or sisters?
How many of you are called to be loving friends?
How many of you have been baptized? You see, a little water goes a long way!

Well, all of you cuckoos and weiner-schnitzels qualify. Welcome to your first day of class. Before you sit down, though, you must take the prophetic oath. Please respond "We do."

Do you believe in the good news of salvation?

All:	We do!
Otto:	Do you believe that there is never life without death, nor death without life?
All:	We do!
Otto:	Do you wish to build your lives and your hopes and dreams on the good news revealed in Jesus Christ?
All:	We do!
Otto:	Do you wish to proclaim this good news by all you say and all you do?
All:	We do!
Otto:	Good! I now pronounce you apprentice prophets! Please sit down. Oooops! Wait a minute folks. I made a boo-boo! I do it everytime. I forgot to read the small print of the prophetic oath. Please stay standing. However, for this part all you have to do is simply nod your heads. These are just a few minor contractual agreements.

Are you prepared to be called cuckoos and have everyone think you are from Switzerland where they make cuckoo clocks? Are you ready to "bite the proverbial bullet" now and then and deny yourselves?
Are you prepared to follow in the footsteps of our founder J. C. Emmanuel and take up your cross everyday?
Are you willing to lose your life in order to save it?

I don't see so many nods, cuckoos. You're not

going to let the small print bother you, are you? And so we continue with more of the tiny-type.

Are you prepared to be manhandled and persecuted?
Are you willing to be sent to prison?
Are you prepared to be brought to trial before state, federal and supreme court justices?
Are you prepared to be rejected and delivered up by parents, relatives, family and friends?
Are some of you even prepared to die? *(Gesture the congregation to be seated.)*

Now don't be frightened by the small print, cuckoos. It's like Skylab falling. The odds are against it happening to you, but just be prepared for "I told you so!" if it does.

Now, without further ado, I would like to introduce the Professor of Criticism, Gert Bonk, with our able assistant, *(mime's name).*

Gert: Thank you, Headmaster. I would like to begin by clearing up a few misunderstandings about what it means to be a prophet. Follow my assistant in the use of that frightful forefinger, also known as the prophetic pointer and apodictic digit.

Most of you thought that what a prophet had to say was either a threat *(mime points her extended forefinger right at the congregation)* or a promise *(mime holds finger straight up in the air in the gesture of an oath)* or a reproach *(mime uses the finger in a sweeping gesture beginning at her left shoulder and moving out and down to her right hip)* or finally, an admonition *(mime wiggles finger by breaking wrist and elbow as finger wags between the congregation and her head).* Well, numbskulls, if this is what you thought it meant to be a prophet, you are wrong! Prophets are called to criticize, to energize and proclaim God's Word. They must give it flesh and blood expression as only they can.

As prophets, then, we are called to espouse a religion of God's freedom and a politics of justice and compassion rather than a religion of imperial order and triumph and a politics of oppression. As prophets we are often called to criticize both the unjust order and the oppression that often numbs people. But the big question is this: What does our criticism consist of?

Now many of you think that to criticize means to rant *(mime begins demonstrating)* and rave, to not stand still for a lot of nonsense, to raise a holy ruckus, to use your best karate and kung-fu to beat the stuffing out of the oppressors for all the evil plots they perpetrate. Right? *(Mime nods her head and smiles gleefully.)*

Well, you're absolutely wrong! *(Mime is shocked.)*

Your prophetic criticism must consist not in carping or denouncing, but in asserting that the false claims of authority and power cannot keep their promises. Your criticism must consist in your capacity and ability to grieve. For grief is the most visceral announcement that things are not right. You must bring yours and your people's hurt to public expression. Prophetic criticism, then, consists in your ability *(here the mime helps again)* to be compassionate, to cry out with others because you experience and stand in their pain. It means the readiness to care *(some gesture)*, to suffer *(some gesture)*, to die *(some gesture)* and to feel *(some gesture)*. And for all of you, the ultimate criticism must be experienced and embodied in the cross.

So now do you see that rather than being called to rant and rave *(mimed again)*, you are called to be people who are compassionate *(gesture)*, people who have the power to care *(gesture)*, the capacity to weep *(gesture)*, the energy to grieve *(gesture)* and the faith to believe that there is never life without death *(gesture)* nor death without life *(gesture of the cross)*.

Otto: Thank you, Gert, for your enlightening remarks. However, criticism alone would be a dead end. It would be disastrous. Prophets are also called to energize. So right now I would like to introduce our Professor of Energy, Ms. Rosie Daifter. Take it away, Rosie.

Rosie: Thank you, Otto. Don't you just love people with German accents? The prophet can often feel like he or she is running out of gas. I mean all that suffering and dying can be a devastating experience. And before we go any further, I think we should listen to the prophet Ezekiel, who with the assistance of the choir can help us all understand how God can draw out new life from old dry bones.

(Here the choir sings "Dry Bones" or a recording of this is played.)

So how does a prophet energize? With the assistance of *(mime's name)*, we'll attempt to show you. I'll bet a lot of you think that it would give the prophet and the people a boost if the prophet just blasted or devastated the order that oppresses: busting a few heads *(mimed)*, breaking a few arms of injustice, giving it to the bad guys and wacko women like they do in all those "B" movies of the fifties and sixties. Right? *(Mime nods confidently.)* Well, you're wrong again, tinkle-brains! *(Mime is devastated.)*

The prophet energizes the people by first having a dream and then teaching others to dream. As prophets you must help people embrace hope. You energize people by helping them believe again, by telling the "old story" of God's faithfulness and love again and again since we all have such short memories. As prophets you are called to bring the people right around you — husbands, wives, family, friends, neighbors, the people you work and play with — to engage the promise of newness that is at work in our history with God. And this is where you can see the connection between criticizing and energizing with the assistance of *(mime's name)*. Newness comes from expressed pain *(gesture)*; suffering made audible and visible produces hope *(gesture)*; articulated grief is the gate of newness *(gesture)*. As Christians, as prophets, we must grow to appreciate and experience that Resurrection is the ultimate act of prophetic energizing in which a new history is initiated *(grand gesture here)*.

Otto: Thank you, Rosie. And now we must hear from our third and final professor. She is our Professor of Uniquity, Ms. Bea Urself.

Bea: What I have to say is more easily said than done. We don't become different people just because we are prophets. Amos was a shepherd and a forester until the day he died. Don't forget that Moses was shy, Judith was a widow, Isaiah was a little boy, Jeremiah stuttered, Deborah had to lead timid, disbelieving men, and on and on.
Often when we look at other people's gifts we become blinded to our own. But each of us is given

God's Word. We are called to proclaim and express that Word, that Good News, by all we say and all we do. And most importantly, we are called to proclaim God's Good News with our gifts. God wants to speak to those around us through our hearts, our feelings, our thoughts, our faces, our voices and personalities, our gifts of laughter and tears. So, as you continue your prophetic ministry, continue to try and feel your sister's and brother's disasters and disappointments. Believe in yourself and help others to believe in their imagination, their hopes, their dreams. If prophecy means anything, it means speaking the Word of God where we are, to those we find ourselves with, in the only ways we know how to speak it. So let the Word continue to become flesh in your lives, in your world. And you don't have to go to far off distant lands in order to let this happen. The hardest places to do this are those closest to you: in your home, in your office, in your school, in your government and in your church. Thank you.

Otto: Thank you, Bea. You have now completed the course work, cuckoos. Now it is time for your final examination. So please stand and with the assistance of *(mime's name)* demonstrate your prophetic knowledge. Don't forget that your participation is important and necessary for the successful completion of your course work.

As prophets you will be occasionally called upon to perform symbolic actions. You must be able to embody criticism and energy in your own unique ways. Your final exam consists in following *(mime's name)* as best you can.

First of all, did you learn what it doesn't mean to be a prophet? Well, let's see if you remember. Remember that the prophet is not just called to threaten, to promise, to reproach and admonish *(gestures to the above with the forefinger)*.

Secondly, do you remember how, as prophets, you must criticize not by ranting and raving but experiencing and embodying the cross? *(Gesture)* Good.

Thirdly, do you recall how, as prophets, you will energize your people? Will you share your hopes *(gesture)* and dreams *(gesture)* and faith in resurrection *(gesture)*? Good.

And lastly, in your own unique ways will you continue to witness to our Christian paradox and mystery: that there is never life without death *(gesture)* nor death without life *(gesture)*? Excellent!

I am happy to announce that you have all successfully passed the course and are ready to graduate. You will receive your diplomas at communion. But now please remain standing for the commencement address which will be delivered today by the founder of our Prophet-Sharing School, J. C. Emmanuel.

Celebrant: The Lord be with you.

All: And also with you.

Celebrant: This is from the Good News according to Mark. (Mk. 6:7-13)

All: Glory to you, Lord.

Celebrant: I am sending you out two by two, and giving you authority over unclean spirits. Take nothing on the journey but a walking stick. Take no food, no travelling bag, and no money in your purse or wallet. You may wear shoes, but do not take a change of clothes. Whatever house you find yourself in, stay there until you leave the locality. If any place will not receive you or hear you, shake its dust from your feet in testimony against them as you leave. So go now, when you leave here today, and preach the need for repentance. Expel many demons, anoint the sick with oil, and work all sorts of cures.

And this is the Good News of the Lord.

All: Praise to you, Lord Jesus Christ. *(All sit.)*

Finis

Theme: What does it mean to be a prophet?

Scripture: Isaiah 42:6-8 *(I have called you to serve the cause of right.)* or
Micah 6:8 *(What the prophet is called to.)*

Props: 1. One recording of "Dry Bones."

2. Three placards: one reading "Good Morning, Professor," another reading "Right," and a third reading "No."

76

3. Four costumes for the members of the Prophet-Sharing School staff. These will be mentioned under production notes.

Production Notes: This dramatization was originally performed at the Oakland Cathedral as part of their summer series on Prophet-Sharing.

This particular liturgical dramatization incorporates two of the readings from the lectionary for the fifteenth Sunday of the year.

The dramatization calls for five characters. This does not include the reader and the celebrant who also have roles to play. The mime leads the congregation in different movements and at other times embodies what is being said. While some specific suggestions are made in the script, much is left to the imagination of the particular mime.

The Headmaster, Otto Von Stoop, can use a German accent if he is able. It adds a somewhat comedic effect. The other professors can use whatever voice or accent seems appropriate. The Professor of Uniquity, however, should be plain and straightforward. The script is written in plain English to avoid phonetic confusion for the reader. No accents have to be used. You might like to play with the idea, however.

Each character should wear something appropriate to the person they are portraying. For instance, Otto von Stoop should wear a graduation cap and gown.

At communion time all are invited to come up for their diplomas even if they do not wish to share the bread and wine.

If you have an organist or piano player you might consider "Pomp and Circumstance" as the recessional or closing song.

Study Questions

1. What is a prophet? Who were some prophets or prophetesses of old? What type of people were they? What type of person was Amos? Can you think of any modern day men and women who are prophetic? Who are they? Where do they live? What do they do? How are they prophetic?

2. What are some of the ordinary ways that every Christian is called to be prophetic? How are you called to be prophetic through what you say and what you do? Is it easy to be a prophet? Is it important?

3. Take a closer look at the prophetic oath, both the large and small print. Go through it question by question. How can we honestly live and embody this by the quality of our lives? What will be some of the harder parts to live out? Why? What can help us live them fully? Explore and discuss.

4. What does oppression mean? What are oppressive structures? Can you name any? Have you ever felt oppressed? How? Think hard, now, and reflect on whether you have ever oppressed others by your attitude, your words or your actions. If you have, how could you change this?

5. Reflect on the passage from the prophet Micah (6:8). What does it mean to act justly? What are ways you do act justly? Are there areas of your life where you could act more justly? What would these be? How would you go about this? What about becoming more conscious of and sensitive to the needs of the world? What does it mean to love tenderly? What obstacles keep you from loving this way? How can you creatively deal with them? What does it mean to walk humbly with God? Explore and discuss.

6. How are we called to criticize as prophets? What does it mean to be compassionate? How are we called to be compassionate? Is this easy or hard? Why? How is the ultimate criticism for all prophets experienced and embodied in the cross? Explore and discuss. (An excellent treatment of compassion and its implications can be found in Matthew Fox's book *A Spirituality Named Compassion.*)

7. How are we called to energize as prophets? What do you hope for? Share some of your dreams. Why are hopes and dreams so important? How can you help other people dream dreams? How can you help others embrace hope? How do you tell the story of God's faithfulness and love over and over again? Explore and discuss how many ways you can come up with. How and why is the resurrection the ultimate act of prophetic energizing?

8. Do we become different people because we are prophets? What is God's Good News? How do we proclaim this with our particular gifts? How can we proclaim and embody God's Word where we are? What are some of the difficulties we will encounter from ourselves and others? How can we deal with these? Does Jesus' life, his words and example offer us any help? How?

The Journey Of The Ark

Cast:

Narrator	Owl
Noah	Peacock
God	Donkey
Raven	Cuckoo
Kangaroo	Gorilla
Butterfly	Turkey
Chicken	Baby Kangaroos (2)
Lamb	Bee

Narrator: A long, long time ago, God decided to send a flood on the earth. Floods, as you know, are powerful. They can destroy. But they can also cleanse, refresh and renew dried, parched earth. God was aware of all that the flood might do to the earth, so he told his friend Noah to build an ark which would house a male and female of every living species. The ark would also house Noah, his wife and their family.

After months and weeks of preparation, the ark was completed. Noah and his family had gathered all the animals. Imagine bringing all of those different kinds of animals together! Noah was desperately trying to get them all into the ark. He was just about at wits' end when he noticed God sitting underneath the shade of a tree watching all of the clamor and confusion. And God was laughing. Noah finally went over to him.

Noah: Excuse me, Sir, but what do you think is so funny?

God: I never dreamed how noisy and confusing such a gathering could be.

Noah: Well, Sir, you may find it amusing, but I do not! Look at them all. How am I going to get all of them into that ark? Do you see the size of those elephants and rhinos? Look at those giraffes. How am I going to get them into the ark without breaking their necks? I'm surprised that the little

81

	critters haven't been stomped to death yet. I mean, Sir, if you don't mind my saying, this is not my idea of a good time or a bad time for that matter!
God:	You're right, Noah! It was my idea!
Noah:	But what am I to do? I don't see how it can ever work.
God:	Trust me, Noah. I helped you build the ark. I enabled you to get all the animals here. I will be with you on your journey. Just remember, I was the architect. I know what I am doing. Trust me!
Narrator:	So Noah just bowed his head in assent and shook it in disbelief. Then Noah returned to the gathering of animals where chaos reigned. All the creatures were at close quarters. Some of the animals like the turkey the donkey and the cuckoo were getting claustrophobic. They quickly worked themselves and the other animals into a loud and nervous frenzy. Noah finally tried to quiet them.
Noah:	All right, you creatures, stifle the noises. I said stifle the noises! Now what's all the racket about?
Raven:	Well, captain, some of us are not too happy with the way thing are going. Many of us don't like our lodging prospects or our potential next door neighbors.
Chicken:	*(Noise)* I don't like the idea of living next to Clem Coyote.
Lamb:	And I, Lorna Lamb, simply detest the very idea of living next to Leopold Lion.
Raven:	And that's not all. We're all anxious and frightened about what will happen. Most of us think that this ark will never float. It's too bulkly and cumbersome. How do we know there will be enough food? Not everyone eats like a mouse. We have some pretty big animals here with hefty appetites.
Narrator:	But just about this time, one of the bees buzzed in.
Bee:	If you ask me, Raven, there are too many queens around here and not enough drones.
Noah:	Thank you, bee, for your reflections. And now I want to ask all of you animals, large and small, to stop your fighting and complaining. I have many questions and fears, too. But if we don't put aside our fears and help each other to get on the ark in time, we will never escape the disastrous flood.

Raven:	If you ask me, Noah, you're just using scare tactics! How can there be a flood without rain? Why, we haven't felt a drop of rain for...
Narrator:	And before Raven had a chance to complete his sentence, the skies filled with clouds and rain began to fall. Before the animals knew it, they were up to their knees in water. The smaller animals were already over their heads. Gradually the little creatures sought refuge on the backs of the larger animals. Noah once again exhorted them.
Noah:	Please, my little friends, please hurry!
Narrator:	Then something marvelous happened. The bees and ants, convinced of the wisdom in Noah's words and the value of working together, used their sharpened arts of persuasion to speed up boarding on the ark. Animals of all colors, all shapes and all sizes hurriedly boarded the ark. Those who had been many were now one family and their new home was the ark...
	The strength of the storm increased. All the animals held their breath. Many feared the worst. It was the raven, that pesky prophet of doom, who screeched:
Raven:	This ark will never get off the ground! Mark my words!
Narrator:	The animals huddled closer together, shivering, shaking. Then slowly the ark began to float. They didn't sink after all. Suddenly the animals *(all except the raven)* broke into wild rejoicing. They didn't care how slowly the ark moved right now. The ark protected them from the rain, the storm, the flood and certain death. They were dry and safe on the ark.
	Things went well for the first few days. But the raven was angry that no one had listened to him. He began sowing seeds of discontent. One day while Noah was walking and talking with the creatures of the ark, the raven got the owl to inquire:
Owl:	Whoooo's steering this ship, if you please?
Noah:	Why, nobody.
Turkey:	Nobody? Gobble-gobble-gobble. *(The donkey and cuckoo and other animals chime in nervously.)*

Owl:	*(The owl quiets the other animals.)* Well, what direction are we sailing? North, south, east, or west?
Noah:	Yes! *(All the animals are flustered again.)*
Peacock:	If you don't mind my asking, what's our heading?
Noah:	Can't we honestly say. *(All the animals react again.)*
Donkey:	But where are we going?
Noah:	Don't know.
Cuckoo:	When will we get there?
Noah:	When we get there.
Raven:	Oh my God, this man's gone ape!
Gorilla:	*(Dumbish)* What do you mean?
Raven:	I mean he's gone bananas!
Noah:	I have the same questions that all of you have. I told God that this whole adventure seemed preposterous.
Raven:	And what did he say to that?
Noah:	He simply said to trust in him. And if I trust in him, I am going to have to ask all of you to trust in me. At least we're dry and safe in the ark. God willing, before the food runs out and our tempers become too short, we will reach some dry land.
Narrator:	Then the creature from "down under", a wise and gentle kangaroo, spoke up for the first time.
Kangaroo:	Brothers and sisters of our animal family, pause for a moment and reflect on the rashness of Raven's actions and the wisdom of Noah's words. We are all afraid. We are frightened of many things... most of them unknown. But we don't have to let our fears divide us or drive us apart. Let's support one another in our weakness.
Raven:	Don't listen to that jumper's jibberish! You're silly to trust anyone. Look what trusting Noah got you. We'd all be better off on our own. Help yourselves! Remember, charity begins at home.
Kangaroo:	But this is our home, Raven. And if we don't help one another and float together, then we are all destined to sink together.
Narrator:	Heartened by the kangaroo's words the animals again applied themselves to make the best of a bad

situation. But the raven was even more angry since the creatures once again chose not to follow his advice. Now the raven tried to create factions among the animals of the ark. He began by pointing out the obvious differences between the animals. He whispered in the anteater's and elephant's ears what a big stink the skunk created. This offended their sensitive noses and made the skunk very ashamed and self-conscious. The raven also pointed out how some animals like the porcupines had rough edges and kept others at a distance. He next pointed out the less than cleanly habits of the pigs, which offended just about every animal's sensibilities. He drew attention to the continual noise the beavers made with their tails; how the mocking birds would never shut up; and how the hyenas laughed constantly. All of these offended the rabbits who had large, sensitive ears. Factions grew as differences became more obvious. As the journey continued, the animals gradually divided themselves into two groups. Each faction expressed their ark experience in terms of one or another extreme. There were the earthworms who thought they would die any minute and lived in constant dread of this last great catastrophe. They saw their fears justified in the huge waves that continually swept over the ship.

The other camp resembled fluttering butterflies. Where the earthworms could only see misery and destruction, the butterflies could only see beauty and life. They were blinded to the difficulties of the ark and would not let them in. The earthworms grew to detest the butterfly camp as the butterfly camp grew to detest the earthworm faction. The raven was delighted by the state of things and tried to compound the confusion by inciting each group against the other.

Raven: *(To the earthworms)* Look at that butterfly camp.

Are you going to let those pompous preditors compound your misery? Their smiles and laughter mock you and your pain. Why not give them something to moan and groan about themselves? *(The earthworms work themselves up into a frenzy.)*

Kangaroo: Wait just one minute. I have been watching this for days! Are you once again going to let Raven turn you against each other? Can't you see what he has done? Dividing us into factions! What does that accomplish? Are we going to focus on our differences for the rest of this trip and our lives, or what we share in common? Both of your groups are only seeing and experiencing half of life. There is joy and sorrow. There is winter and spring. One flows out of the other. We must live with both if we wish to be whole and healthy animals. So don't just see the bad in each other. See the good too. Take both. If you only look for the bad, that is all you will find. Don't just settle for half of life. Look for and enjoy all of it.

Narrator: And once again the animals came to their senses. And once again the raven was mad. Sorry for what they had done to one another, the animals bowed their heads and gradually asked one another's forgiveness. Weeks passed and the animals grew closer together. But the ornery raven was not finished with the animals yet. As the weeks turned into a month the raven began feeling restless. The confinement was too much for him and he began to get arkal fever. The raven tried one last time to get the animals to reject their situation and be something other than themselves. These were precisely the symptoms of arkal fever.

Raven: Gather round me, all you animals. Maybe now you will listen to what I have to say. Are you tired of being cooped up in here?

Animals: Yes!

Raven: Would you like to do something about it?

Animals: Yes, we would very much!

Raven: Well, you can if you want to!

Turkey: But what?

Raven: You don't have to stay in this ark, none of you! You can leave anytime you want.

Donkey: But how? Most of us can't fly or swim!

Raven: That's what Noah wants you all to believe! You can't fly or swim because you've never tried it. If you want to badly enough, and if you believe in yourselves, you can do anything you want.

Kangaroo: Personally, I would advise against Raven's

86

	suggestion. We said we would trust Noah. Let's be true to our word.
Raven:	Don't listen to that bouncing baboon. She's just full of kangadoo-doo!
Owl:	If it's so easy, Raven, then why don't you go first and show us?
Raven:	Alright, I'll prove it to you once and for all!
Kangaroo:	Please, Raven, you don't have to do this. You could hurt yourself badly and none of us wish to see that happen to you.
Narrator:	But the raven had worked himself up into a frenzy. He was not going to lose face anymore. The giraffe, with its long neck, opened the roof of the ark and let the raven out. Then the raven flew down by the window on the side of the ark. He was playful and free. Just when some of the other animals were ready to climb up the giraffe's neck and out of the ark, a gigantic wave swept the raven into the water. All the animals crowded to the portholes and watched the raven helplessly flounder in the water. He couldn't swim after all, and now he was drowning. The animals were terribly saddened and disturbed.
Turkey:	All is lost! All is lost!
Donkey:	Woe is me! And woe to thee!
Cuckoo:	What can we do? Is everyone too scared to go after poor raven?
Kangaroo:	I'm willing to try. I can bounce high enough to make it up on the roof. Then I can jump in and flip raven back to safety with the strength of my tail.
Narrator:	And that is exactly what Kangaroo did. All the animals watched anxiously. Kangaroo jumped from the roof of the ark into the water. When she reached raven, who was just ready to go under for the third time, she flipped him up to safety. Raven staggered through the opening in the roof. But as Kangaroo attempted to climb back on the ark, a large wave swept over her. She was carried under the water and seen no more.
	What sadness was on the ark. Even the raven was repentent. Noah, who had been unaware of all that happened, came in and discovered the tragic news. After some time he spoke to the sorrowful creatures.

Noah:	My friends, we have been reminded about the gift of life by the selflessness of the Kangaroo. She had the courage not only to say she loved us, but to put her life on the line for that love. She loved not only in word, but in deed.
Narrator:	The Koala bears were so sad. But after a good cry and blowing their noses they went over and comforted the baby Kangaroos which mama Kangaroo had carried around in her pouch. All the animals, including the raven, remembered what the Kangaroo had said. Through her dying, they became more vulnerable to one another. They shared their sorrow and comforted one another. They also grew to love and appreciate one another more openly. They daily grew closer together and found their commitment to one another deepened. If the Kangaroo had loved the raven and them all so much, they wanted to try to love each other in the same way.
	And then one day the rains stopped. There was hushed stillness. Slowly the waters receded and land began appearing. The animals looked at one another in amazement. Then, after some time, Noah came and told them that the glorious time of their departure had arrived. It didn't seem very glorious to any of them.
Noah:	There we go, that does it, the door of the ark is open. It is my distinct privilege to invite you all now to disembark from the ark.
Narrator:	But the animals only huddled together closely.
Noah:	What's the matter?
Owl:	We're afraid, Noah.
Noah:	Afraid of what?
Raven:	Of being alone.
Turkey:	Of not having you with us to solve our problems or give us advice.
Donkey:	We may never again find someone to share life with.
Cuckoo:	If it rains again, what will we do?
Owl:	We are afraid, Noah. We don't want to be selfish or isolated again. We have learned many important things together. We're afraid that once we go our separate ways, we will forget them.

Turkey:	We're afraid of all we must meet out there.
Noah:	My friends, little and big, I share your concerns and fears. But if we stay here, we will not grow. We cannot make an idol of the ark. God did not intend us to live in the ark forever. It was simply our means of getting from where we were to this time and this place.
Butterfly:	Even I, a fluttering old butterfly, have experienced that in my life. The cocoon was also safe and secure for me. It wasn't easy for me to leave it, but I had to. And hard as it was for me to leave, I was glad I did it afterwards.
Narrator:	Slowly but surely, all the other animals began to understand the wisdom of Noah's and the butterfly's words.
Noah:	And remember creatures — we must do this leaving not once but many times in our lives.
Narrator:	Then Noah gave the creatures a final gift.
Noah:	Creatures of the ark, I give you one last gift. Take with you, wherever you go, the power to remember and give thanks. Never forget what Kangaroo did for us all! She showed each of us what it means to live out our love. You all have the power to remember this and give thanks. Pass this gift on from generation to generation.
	Now it is time for you all to go to the four corners of the earth. Carry with you memory and gratitude as you travel on your respective journeys.
Narrator:	And then Noah went to each of the animals, before he sent them on their way, and he embraced them, for he loved each of the creatures very much. And Noah would not let the Raven slip embarrassedly away.
	Slowly the animals made their way to every part of the world. *(Here the animals go to the different parts of the congregation.)* And do you know that the spirit of Noah, the Kangaroo and the creatures of the ark still hovers high over all God's creation and evokes memory and thanks to this very day.

Finis

Theme:	What does it mean to be a Christian?
Scripture:	Genesis 9:1-17 *(I will establish my covenant with you.)*

89

or I John 3:13-19; 23-24 *(This is my commandment: love one another.)*

Props: 1. Costumes that are simple and suggestive of each animal character. Hats with ears or feathers would be fine. Also endeavor to capture the different animal characters through your body movements and walks.

Production Notes: This dramatization was originally performed in a liturgy at Holy Names College in Oakland, CA. It was part of Modern Liturgy's Second Annual Festival of the Lively Arts in Worship. It was commissioned by the publisher of Modern Liturgy, William Burns, for that occasion.

If you decide to have a woman play the role of God, adjust the gender of pronouns referring to God and replace Sir with Madam.

As always, pay close attention to the text for clues about appropriate actions and movements. It is always the dramatic action which will transform these scripts from dramatic readings to dramatic experiences.

Study Questions: 1. Is it easy to take a group of individuals and teach them to live together as a family or community? Why or why not? What are some of the difficulties that you might experience? What are some of the obstacles that must be overcome? How would you deal with these?

2. Did Raven make Noah's job easier or harder? Why? How? What are some of Raven's fears? Have you ever experienced any of them in your own life? Discuss and share.

3. Does Raven change during the course of the journey? How does Raven change? Why does Raven change? Do you change during your journey through life? How do you change? What causes you to change? Do you influence changes in other people? How?

4. What did you think of Kangaroo? What did the other animals think of Kangaroo? How do the Kangaroo's actions speak louder than her words? How does the Kangaroo continue to live on even

after her death? Do people we know, who have died, continue to live on in our lives? How?

5. God invites Noah to trust and believe that God will accompany him on his journey. Does God issue that same invitation and make that same promise to us? Is it hard or easy to trust and believe in God's word? Why? Who or what can help us trust and believe? Discuss.

6. As Christians we are called to move from isolation into community, from selfishness to love, from death to life. How did the animals of the ark experience these different realities in the dramatization? How do you experience these different realities in your life? What is involved in the process of moving from one to the other? Explore and discuss.

7. Noah gave the animals one final gift as they departed the ark. What was it? Are we given those same gifts? How can and do they help us on our journeys? Try and remember some people who are important in your life. Thank God for the gift of their presence in your life.

8. What are some of the concrete ways you could improve your shared life together in either your family, your classroom or your church community? Explore and discuss.

How The Word Became Flesh

Cast:	God the Father	Hezekiah
	God the Mother	Aurora
	God the Child	Barbara
	Michael	Iris
	Gabriel	Hannah
	Raphael	Deodatus

Narrator: Once upon a time, in a place called heaven, God the Father called God the Mother and God the Child together.

God-Mother: What's the matter? You look worried.

God-Father: I am.

God-Mother: What about?

God-Father: I'm concerned about the children of the earth.

God-Child: But why, Father?

God-Father: They are distanced from our love. Many men and women have forgotten who we are. Others have so distorted us that we resemble cold, unfeeling idols.

God-Child: You mean like the golden calf they once worshipped in the desert during the time of Moses?

God-Father: Exactly!

God-Mother: Is that what bothers you most?

God-Father: No. They have forgotten how to share, how to care for each other. They forget that the poor, the lowly and the little ones of the earth are our beloved children and their brothers and sisters. Instead of easing one another's suffering, they only compound it.

God-Child: What can we do?

God-Mother: We need to ask the help of the Council of Angels.

God-Father: Yes, they advised and helped us create the universe.

93

	And they continue to roam the earth caring for all of our people.
God-Mother:	With their help we will again discover how to show all peoples the depth of our love.
Narrator:	And so the family of God called the Council of Angels together. From the four corners of the universe they came: Michael, Gabriel, Raphael, Hezekiah, Aurora, Barbara, Iris, Hannah and Deodatus. When they assembled, God the Mother spoke.
God-Mother:	Welcome, friends. You have helped us constantly express our love for humankind from the beginning of time as they know it. Now we need your counsel and your help again.
Michael:	What's the matter? Is something wrong?
God-Mother:	Yes. The people of earth find it difficult to experience our love.
God-Child:	Their fears and anxieties distance them from it. Their hearts have grown cold. They no longer feel compassion for their brothers and sisters in need.
Iris:	But what can we do?
God-Father:	Give us your counsel. How can we best communicate our love to all those we have created? Help us find the best possible expression. One the children of earth will always remember and be grateful for.
Narrator:	The Council of Angels did not speak for some time. They thought and thought. How could God's love be best communicated? After some time, the angel Aurora spoke.
Aurora:	Since your love is the beginning and end of all that is, since it lights the darkest night and gives rest to those who labor in the heat of day, place your love in the sun's rising and setting. Let men and women marvel at the brilliance and beauty of your love. Call them every morning to remember your love in each sunrise. And as the sun sets in a burst of color on the horizon, let them offer their prayers of thanksgiving that darkness cannot overcome your love, your light.
God-Child:	Well spoken, Aurora, but my Mother and Father have already given humankind both sunrise and sunset.

God-Father:	Yes, Aurora, we are already present in these gifts. Now we want to bind ourselves more intimately to all of our people.
Hezekiah:	I have an idea.
God-Mother:	Then share it with us, Hezekiah.
Hezekiah:	Why not reveal the strength of your love to them?
God-Child:	How would we do that?
Hezekiah:	Through a mountain!
God-Child:	Through a mountain?
Hezekiah:	Yes! Through the biggest, strongest mountain ever created. You have appeared to them before on mountains. If you did it once, you can do it again. Only this time intensify the experience in such a way that they will never forget it.
God-Father:	Men and women take too much delight in sacred objects. I think they would remember the mountain and forget about our love.
Gabriel:	And besides, if you only reveal yourself in strength, how will people ever be able to discover your presence and love in weakness?
God-Mother:	You're right, Gabriel. We must look for a gentler expression of our love.
God-Father:	Yes, I'm afraid that the mountain is too spectacular.
God-Child:	Mountains may be strong, but they have no feeling. The strength of our love needs to be expressed in a more compassionate and understanding way.
Deodatus:	Have you ever thought of an animal?
God-Child:	Animal?
God-Mother:	Whatever do you mean by that, Deodatus?
Deodatus:	Men and women have learned to raise and tame animals. They see in the different animals some very human qualities. Why not express your love for them by creating some fantastically new animal that would demonstrate many aspects of your love?
God-Child:	But how would we go about designing such a creature?
Deodatus:	It only takes a little imagination. Just think how grand it would be, how people from all over the world would take notice of this animal that

95

combined say the humility of the donkey, the astuteness of the cat, the vigilance of the rooster, the serenity of the dove, the fidelity of the dog, the docility of the lamb, the strength and courage of the lion, the wisdom of the owl, the selflessness of the pelican, the beauty and gentleness and healing of the unicorn, together with the eagle's soaring spirit.

God-Child: That sure was a mouthful! But it would be fantastic! What do you think, Mother?

God-Mother: I think it would be too fantastic to believe. Instead of allowing the love and goodness of such a creature into their lives to transform them, I think they would fear it and drive the animal far away from them.

God-Father: So that in the end we would create a monster instead of a creature that could communicate our love.

Barbara: Jumping Jehosaphat! I've got it!

God-Child: What have you got, angel Barbara?

Barbara: I know how you can express your love.

God-Child: How?

Barbara: What do you want the people of the earth to do with your love?

God-Father: Be aware of it.

God-Mother: Accept it.

God-Child: Share it.

Barbara: Right! Now human beings are easily distracted, so we have to get their attention. I think you need something really unusual and spectacular, something they will never forget. What about a visitor from another planet? Their world is too small as it is. I mean, this would blow their minds! Now this extra-terrestrial being could come swooping in on a flying saucer or something. Once the creature has gotten their attention he can then give the humans the secret of how to live in peace and harmony with people throughout the world.

God-Father: You certainly have a flair for the dramatic, Barbara! But I don't think the earth is quite ready for science fiction.

God-Mother:	The children of the earth would be paralyzed with fear rather than attentive to our message.
God-Child:	I think you're right. They might become aware of it in this way, but I doubt whether they would accept it or share it.
God-Mother:	Council of Angels, we love you all dearly. Don't be discouraged because we have not accepted any of your suggestions. Continue to counsel us and help us look for the right expression of our love.
Iris:	Have you ever thought of expressing your love in color?
God-Mother:	What do you mean, Iris?
Iris:	Why not place your love in the sky as a rainbow? Let men and women marvel at its beauty. Let it remind them of your constant presence and love. The rainbow, like your love, brings many colors together into a beautiful and harmonious whole. It is many and yet it is one. It is only when the different colors are brought together that their real beauty is experienced. Let the rainbow stand as a sign of your love for all people. Bind yourself to all humankind through the rainbow.
God-Father:	That is an excellent idea, Iris, but I've already sent the rainbow to the people of the earth as a sign of our convenantal love for them during the days of Noah.
God-Child:	What we need is some way of binding ourselves to them even more closely.
Raphael:	Since there is so much suffering on earth, and since all men and women are wounded in one way or the other, why not express your love in healing?
God-Mother:	An excellent idea, Raphael! But how?
Raphael:	Your expression must be simple, it must be clear and it must be refreshing. Why not express your love as water? Water can quench the thousand thirsts of humankind. It can cleanse their wounds. It clears blinding dust from weary eyes. And when people gaze into a clear pool of water, they can see the reflection of God's love.
God-Child:	Living water, refreshing water, healing water. That is superb!
God-Father:	You have put us on the right track, Raphael, but

there must be more. Men and women are not only thirsty. They hunger too.

Hannah: Then may I speak?

God-Mother: Of course, Hannah. What have you to add?

Hannah: Since humankind is hungry, why not express your love for them in food that satisfies their hunger?

God-Child: But how?

Hannah: Long ago you gave their ancestors bread in the desert. Why not feed them with bread again? Surely they will remember where the bread comes from and what it represents!

God-Father: Not necessarily.

Hannah: Then perhaps you could express your love through a fruit tree or a vine. Yes, that's it, a vine! A grape vine. The fruit of the vine would be succulent and sweet. It would satisfy their hunger. And from the meat of the grape they could make drink which could quench their thirst and bring joy and exuberance to their lives.

God-Child: What a tremendous idea!

God-Father: But would it be clear? Do you think they would understand?

Michael: While these are all excellent suggestions, they raise a serious question for me. Are men and women ready to see or understand or accept your love in water, in bread, in fruit or wine? I don't think so. They would appreciate these gifts, but I am not at all convinced that they would get to the love that created them and for which they stand.

God-Child: Then how do you propose that we express our love, Michael?

Michael: In the way you have from the beginning of time. Send them a prophet or a prophetess.

God-Father: We have sent them prophets and prophetesses before, Michael, and they have abused them, killed them or dismissed them as insane.

Michael: But there were always a few who saw you and heard your words through them. Let a prophet proclaim your Word in a new and powerful way. I know this would turn people's hearts back to your love again.

God-Father:	I'm just not sure. These are all excellent suggestions. But no single one captures what we want to express. There must be some way.
God-Mother:	There is. And only now do I understand and see what we must do.
God-Father:	What is it that you see?
God-Mother:	We need an expression that encompasses not one but all of these suggestions. Any one of them might be dismissed. People can ignore the beauty of sunrise and the splendor of sunsets. They can excuse or distort the strength of mountains. They can dismiss the giftedness of animals. They can forget the beauty of the rainbow and fail to look beyond the satisfaction of food and drink to the love that created them. They can be blind to the prophet's presence and deaf to the prophet's words.
God-Child:	All of this is depressing, Mother. What could possibly express our love?
God-Mother:	A person could! I think they would let a person into their lives. A human being just like them could help them remember and give thanks.
God-Father:	You mean send our love as a person?
God-Mother:	Yes! And more than that. I think we need to send men and women what we treasure most. It is the best possible gift we could give them.
God-Father:	You mean send them our child?
God-Child:	What an excellent idea!
God-Mother:	Let us send the child in our own image and likeness. In this way, whenever the people of the earth see him, they will see us. Like the sunrise and sunset he will bring life and light and hope. Like the mountain he will share his strength. But it will be the strength of all he feels, all that is human and good and God-like. He will share the laughter and tears, the joys and fears of all people and help them find us in them. Like the rainbow he will be a constant sign and reminder of our love for them. He will be food to feed their hunger and drink to quench their thirst. He will be healing and refreshment. Like the prophets of old he will proclaim our Word, but in a new and powerful way. For he will not just speak to all men and

99

	women about our love. He will be our love for them.
God-Father:	But who will care for him while he is away from us?
God-Mother:	Another mother and another father and later his brothers and sisters, men and women throughout the world.
God-Father:	But how will we give our love, our child, to them?
God-Mother:	We must allow our love to become flesh and blood, a person on earth. Do you agree, my child?
God-Child:	Oh yes, Mother. Yes, Father, with all my heart.
God-Father:	To whom shall we send him?
God-Mother:	I have examined the women of the earth and know of one young girl who is aware of our love. She will be frightened. She will have her doubts. But I believe she will accept him and share him with others.
God-Father:	How will we ask her?
God-Mother:	I would like to send Gabriel to her. He will understand her own amazement. His gentle strength will calm and reassure the young girl that there is nothing to be afraid of.
God-Father:	Then let it be as you have said.
God-Child:	Yes, as you have said, let it be.
Narrator:	And so this is how the Council of Angels helped the family of God decide how they could best express their love to the people on earth. They would allow their love to become flesh and live with them. So they dispatched Gabriel. In the sixth month the angel Gabriel was sent from God to a town of Galilee named Nazareth, to a virgin betrothed to a man named Joseph, of the house of David. The virgin's name was Mary.

Finis

Theme:	How love is expressed.
Scripture:	I John 4:1-13; 19-21 *(Anyone who loves God must love his brother/sister.)* or I Corinthians 13:1-13 *(The importance of love.)*
Props:	None are required.

Production Notes: This was originally done as a Christmas dramatization. It obviously deals with Jesus as the expression of God's love for us.

Slides can be used effectively in this dramatization. As each angel counsels the family of God, pictures of sunrises, sunsets, mountains, food, drink, and so on can be projected onto a screen. They are not necessary, however.

Costuming should be ordinary dress or something else appropriate. Avoid the stereotypical wings for each angel. By avoiding the wings you enhance your chances of reinforcing that all creation reveals and communicates God's love.

Study Questions: 1. What does the word angel mean? What did angels do? How is God's presence and love communicated to us today? Explore and discuss.

2. What are the different angels' names? What does each name mean? Does each angel's suggestion have anything to do with their name? What? What does your name mean? Given the world we live in, do you have any suggestions on ways God could reveal love for us today? Can we help this happen in any way? How?

3. What is God the Father concerned about? Do you find it hard to share? Why or why not? Do you feel one with or connected with the poor, the lowly, the little ones of the earth? Why or why not? What could help me look on every person as my brother or sister? Would this be hard or difficult to do? Why or why not? Is it important? Why or why not?

4. St. Ignatius of Loyola once said that love must be expressed not just in words but in deeds. Is it easier to say "I love you" than to show your love by the way you treat others? Ignatius also said that love consists in a mutual sharing between the ones in love. What does God share with or give to us? How does God do this? What can we share with God? How can we continue to express this in our daily living? Explore and discuss.

5. How do you love other people? How do you express your love for them? What are some of the ways you act or things you do when you want to communicate your love for someone? How do

others express their love for you? What are the ways they act or things they do that communicate their love to you? Why does love need to be expressed? Explore and discuss.

6. What are some of the experiences that you have had that revealed God's presence and love to you in some special way? What was there about these experiences that did this for you? Could you speak of these as God experiences?

7. Who are some of the people in your life who have revealed God's presence and love to you in some special way? What was there about these people that did this for you? Could we refer to them as God persons? How can we be clearer signs of God's love and presence in our world? Explore and discuss.

8. Look at St. John's first letter. What are the ways St. John tells us we can be sure that God's love is in us? Can we really love God and still ignore the needs of our neighbors? Why or why not? Jesus, in the gospels, asks us to love one another as he has loved us. How has Jesus loved us? What are some of the ways that we can express our love for one another?

THE WAY OF JESUS

4

The Temptations

Cast:	Jesus	Crowd-1
	Jesus' Manager	Crowd-2
	Billzee Bub	Announcer
	Billzee's Manager	Placard Holder

(After the proclamation of the Scripture — Luke 4:1-13 — and some silence, the placard holder comes to the center and holds up a placard reading "The Temptations." The placard holder moves away and a recording of the singing group "The Temptations" comes on doing their rendition of "Snake in the Grass." After a few moments a voice yells "No! Not those temptations! The other ones!" The placard holder comes back and holds up the placard once again. The placard holder then leaves. The theme song from "Rocky" comes on. Down the aisle comes Billzee Bub in robe and fighting gear. He and his manager set up in their corner. Next comes the announcer who looks around for Jesus. Finally, Jesus' manager comes up the aisle dragging Jesus. The bell rings.)

Announcer: Ladies and gentlemen, this is the main event. This three round contest is for the championship of the world. In the dark corner, in red trunks and weighing in at a svelte 113 pounds — (to Billzee) only 113 pounds?

Billzee: Oh well! *(Gives a shrug of shoulders.)*

Announcer: Weighing 113 pounds, that Lord of the flies and Prince of Darkness, Billzee Bub!

Billzee: *(He comes out of his corner as the placard holder lifts a card reading "BOO.")*

Announcer: And in the light corner, wearing transfiguration white trunks, and led by the spirit, weighing 155 pounds *(put here whatever the actual weight of your Jesus character is)*, a relative unknown just beginning his career, Jesus of Nazareth.

Jesus: *(He comes out of his corner as the placard holder lifts a card reading "HOORAY.")*

Announcer:	(The two fighters meet in the center of the ring.) Now let's have a fair fight. No blows below the belt. No cheating. No lying. No gouging or biting. Agreed?
Jesus:	Agreed!
Billzee:	(The announcer looks at him.) I have a confession to make. I lied. I don't weigh 113 pounds. I weigh 114 pounds.
Jesus:	But what about the agreement?
Billzee:	(He just shrugs his shoulders.)
Announcer:	O.K. Now go to your corners and come out fighting.
	(They go to their corners. Billzee's corner freezes. Jesus comes alive and begins praying earnestly on one knee. Jesus' corner freezes as Billzee's corner comes alive.)
Billzee:	What should I use for my first move?
B-Manager:	Hit him with the old "stones into bread" routine.
Billzee:	That tired old number? That will never work!
Crowd-1:	Oh yes it will! He's got hungers just like the rest of us. Get him to hunger for our affirmation!
B-Manager:	Get him to doubt himself!
Crowd-1:	Tire him out! Get him to constantly prove his self-worth!
B-Manager:	Confuse him!
Crowd-1:	Convince him to do spectacular things or no one will believe in him!
B-Manager:	No one will accept him!
Billzee:	Fine! Say no more.
	(The placard holder shows a card reading "Round One." The bell rings. Jesus gets off of one knee and blesses himself. Jesus and Billzee move to the center of the ring. They joust around and throw a few fake punches.)
Billzee:	Who are you anyway?
Jesus:	I'm a child of God.
Billzee:	Oh yeah? Well if you're a child of God, then turn those stones over there into bread.

	(Billzee gets Jesus to look away and begins to throw a punch. Billzee freezes as Jesus steps out.)
Jesus:	You know, it might work.
J-Manager:	Don't listen to him!
Crowd-2:	Don't you see what he's doing to you?
J-Manager:	He's trying to confuse you. If he gets you to prove yourself once, he'll get you to do it a hundred times.
Crowd-2:	Changing stones today, moving mountains tomorrow. There will be no end to it!
J-Manager:	You know who you are!
Crowd-2:	Believe in yourself!
Jesus:	That's right!
	(Jesus steps back into place and the action resumes with Billzee throwing his punch. Jesus fends off Billzee's punch and delivers one of his own lines before hitting Billzee with a punch of his own.)
Jesus:	Not by bread alone do people live, but by every word that comes from the mouth of God.
	(Jesus delivers his punch. The bell rings. Billzee wanders dazedly to Jesus' corner. J-Manager points Billzee to his own corner. A bird whistle toots in the background. Billzee wanders to his corner as Jesus returns to his.)
Billzee:	Thanks a lot! Any other bright ideas?
B-Manager:	Yeah! You're building up his confidence. That's great! The higher he gets, the harder he'll fall. When you've got him where you want him, try the "power play" gamut on him.
Billzee:	You've got to be kidding! Wake up and smell the coffee! That can't work!
Crowd-1:	Yes it can! Convince him that only if he says and does the right things will people follow him.
B-Manager:	Confuse him! Get him to live up to people's expectations.
Crowd 1:	Tire him out with fear and anxiety of rejection.
Billzee:	Alright! I think I've got him now.
	(The placard person displays a card reading "Round Two." The bell rings. Jesus blesses himself again. Jesus and Billzee met at center ring. They spar briefly.)

Billzee: You know, kid, you've got class. You laid some pretty smooth moves on me last round. The people loved you. They're ready for more. You know something, you could learn a lot from me. I can help you go places. I can give you the world. And all you've got to do is go down. Take one little dive.

(Billzee throws a punch after saying this and freezes. JESUS STEPS OUT.)

Jesus: That's tempting.

J-Manager: Don't listen to him! He's no good! He's just trying to manipulate you!

Crowd-2:   He just wants you to give up control of your life. He has no power, no real authority to give you.

J-Manager: Be true to yourself, kid! That's where real power lies.

Crowd-2:   Give in now and you'll be making concessions for the rest of your life.

J-Manager: Power isn't out there. It's inside of you!

(Jesus steps back into his place. The action resumes. Billzee continues with his punch. Jesus blocks it and says the following line before delivering a blow that rocks Billzee.)

Jesus: You must worship the Lord and serve God alone.

(Billzee staggers and spits out some teeth — these are popcorn kernels — as the bell rings. Billzee goes to his corner as Jesus goes to his.)

Billzee: I only have one thing to say. "Finito!" I'm not going back out there!

B-Manager: Don't be silly! You've got him worried. He's second guessing himself.

Billzee: I beg your pardon? He's worried? I'm worried!

B-Manager: I think he's ready for the big one.

Billzee: What do you mean?

B-Manager: The "take-him-to-the-top" trick.

Billzee: Huh?

Crowd-1:   He's overconfident now.

B-Manager: Yeah! Get him to believe that God's on his side.

Crowd-1:   Get him to believe that nothing can go wrong.

B-Manager:	Yeah! If God's on his side then nothing can happen to him!
Crowd-1:	Get him to doubt his humanity!
B-Manager:	Get him to doubt his divinity!
Crowd-1:	And then lower the boom!
B-Manager:	And don't let up when he's down! Pour it on!
Billzee:	Alright! Sold, my man!
	(The placard holder shows a card reading "Round Three." The bell rings. Jesus blesses himself in his corner before coming to the center ring. Billzee meets Jesus at center ring and they begin sparring.)
Billzee:	You know, kid everything is going your way. I don't think I can throw anything at you that you can't handle. You're riding real high. You've got the crowd and this fight in the palm of your hand. Hey! Did you see those three kings over there?
	(Jesus looks in the direction that Billzee points. Billzee then punches him and knocks him to the floor. Billzee stands over him laughing. Then Billzee goes over to his manager. During this entire sequence, the announcer steps near to Jesus and begins a knockdown count in slow motion.)
Billzee:	Solid! Give me five! He was gettin' too tall! He was ready for a fall!
	(Billzee returns to a position over Jesus on the floor.)
Billzee:	You put your trust in God, kid. What good did it do you? If this God of yours is so great, where is he now? Are you finally ready to let go of all that "greasy kid stuff"? It's your last chance, kid. You stick with me and I can take you to the top.
J-Manager:	Don't listen to him.
Crowd-2:	You don't test God.
J-Manager:	You got sloppy, kid. But it's not the end of the world.
Crowd-2:	God's with you, even when you're down.
J-Manager:	Remember, his power works best in your weakness!
Crowd-2:	Draw strength from your faith.
J-Manager:	And your faith is strongest when it's based on trust.
Crowd-2:	Believe that God's with you!

Billzee:	You deserve better treatment than this, kid!
	(Jesus slowly gets up.)
Jesus:	You're right! And I think I can do something about that now.
Billzee:	Stay down, kid. Everyone will understand. Alright, then maybe we can play this scenario another way. You know that you're not competition tough yet. You make beginners' mistakes. If I hadn't helped you by taking a dive in the first round and putting my guard down in the second, you'd never have gotten this far. But have it your way. I'll let you win. I'll go down for the count. But remember, I let you win! Are you sure you won't reconsider?
	(Billzee swings at Jesus. Jesus blocks his haymaker punch and delivers the following line before knocking Billzee out.)
Jesus:	Scripture says you don't put God to the test.
Announcer:	One. Five. Seven. Ten. You're out!
	(Billzee's manager comes and drags Billzee back to his corner. The announcer raises Jesus' hand.)
Announcer:	The winner, by a knock-out in the third round, Jesus of Nazareth.
	(There are loud cheers and applause. The placard holder may raise a card reading "Applause." Then Jesus goes to Billzee's corner and extends his hand in a gesture of sportsmanship.)
Billzee:	It's not over, kid. You know that, don't you?
Jesus:	What do you mean?
B-Manager:	He means that you may have won the battle, but you're going to lose the war.
Billzee:	I mean we'll meet again, at the appointed time.
	(All characters freeze. After a few moments they turn their backs to the congregation and freeze in this position for a few moments. Then they turn and go to their places.)

Finis

Theme:	God's supportive presence even in the midst of trial and temptation.
Scripture:	Luke 4:1-13 *(The temptations of Jesus in the desert.)*
	or
	Isaiah 43:1-7 *(Call to trust in God.)*

110

Props:	1. One recording of "Snake in the Grass" by The Temptations.
	2. One recording of the theme from "Rocky."
	3. One bell.
	4. Two pairs of boxing gloves.
	5. Two boxing outfits *(we used shorts, shirts, shoes, socks, and robes).*
	6. Two towels.
	7. Two stools.
	8. One bird whistle.
	9. One handful of popcorn kernels.
	10. Seven placards that read: The Temptations — Boo — Hooray — Applause — Round One — Round Two — and Round Three.

Production Notes:

This dramatization was originally performed at the Pacific School of Religion as part of a liturgy for the first Sunday in Lent. It is light but meaty. This was an attempt to invite the people to enter into the transformative experience of Lent joyfully and not morosely.

There is no actual ring for the fight. The two stools and the position of the managers will help establish the confines of the ring.

The two characters named Crowd-1 and Crowd-2 are situated in the congregation on the opposite side of the corner they are interacting with. This is an attempt to bring the congregation into the drama more effectively as well as situating the temptations where they actually occur.

The placard holder should also do the sound effects.

It is important that the boxing between Jesus and Billzee be simple and choreographed. It is stylized. If the characters move around too much or are too frenetic in their movements, important pieces of the dialogue will be lost.

Study Questions:

1. What are some of the things you hunger for? Do you hunger for the affirmation of others? How do

you go about getting the affirmation of others? What are some constructive and helpful ways? What ways would be destructive or unhelpful? Do you have self doubts? What are some of them? Reflect and share.

2. Do you agree with Jesus' manager that if you begin proving yourself, there is no end to it? Why or why not? What are some of the ways you try to prove your self worth or value? Are these ultimately satisfying or frustrating? Why? What does it mean "to believe in yourself?" How do you go about believing in yourself? Explore and discuss.

3. What does Jesus mean when he says that people are nourished by every word that comes from the mouth of God? Have you ever felt strengthened or helped by God's word? What are some of these words that come from God's mouth? What piece or pieces of scripture have supported and sustained you most? Share these. Since Jesus is God's Word in the flesh, who are some of the other living and breathing words of God who help you grow? How do they do this?

4. Do you ever find yourself living up to the expectations of others? What are some of those expectations? Is this type of living satisfying or frustrating? Why do people try to live up to the expectations of others? What expectations do you have of yourself? What do you want? What kind of person do you want to become? Do you think God has any expectations of us? If so, what would some of those be? Did Jesus in his words or actions give us any indication about the kind of people God would like us to become? What would these indications be?

5. Do you agree that real power lies in being true to yourself? Why or why not? What does it mean to be true to yourself? What are some examples of being true to yourself? What would be some examples of not being true to yourself? What type of power does Jesus talk about in his own life? What is the difference between "power over" and "power for," between domination and cooperation or service? What does Jesus call us to? What are some obstacles to genuine service of others? Can you think of some creative ways to deal with these?

6. What does Jesus mean when he says we must worship the Lord and serve God alone? What are some of the things in life that we make into gods and serve? Reflect on this and share.

7. What is the difference between presumption and faith? How does faith find expression in someone's life? How would presumption be expressed? Find a recording of Bob Dylan's "With God on our Side" and listen to it. What are some of the injustices that he sings about where people have presumed God was on their side? Jesus tells us that God is on the side of the poor, the lowly, the hungry and thirsty, the naked, those in prison and alone. Can you identify with these people? What would be some creative ways to develop compassion for all the people of the world who fall into these categories? Can we presume that God is really on our side if we cannot understand and identify with them? Why or why not? Explore and discuss.

8. Look at a United States coin and read the phrase "In God We Trust." Do you think that as a nation we actually trust in God? Why or why not? Do you trust in God? How do you show this or reveal this in your life? What are some of the ways you test God? Read Isaiah 43:1-7. Have you ever experienced God's presence when you were down? When and how? Do you believe God's power can work best in your weakness? Why or why not? If you believe it can, how can it?

Turning Point

Cast:	Narrator	Man-1
		Man-2
	Jesus	Man-3
	Reporter-1	Man-4
	Reporter-2	Man-5
	Jack Horner	Man-6
	Rose	Woman-1
	Cousin	Woman-2
	Lame Person	Woman-3
	Gentile	Woman-4

Narrator: A reading from the Good News according to Luke. Jesus returned in the power of the Spirit to Galilee, and his reputation spread throughout the region. He was teaching in their synagogues, and all were loud in his praise.

He came to Nazareth where he had been reared...

Reporter-1: Are we on?

Reporter-2: No. We've got about thirty seconds.

Reporter-1: Alright, Jimmy, for once let's try to keep it tight.

Reporter-2: Anything you say, dearie.

Reporter-1: I'll start with a brief introduction, then throw it to you for some penetratingly insightful remarks. You then give it back to me in the front of the synagogue to find out what the religious leaders and some of the prominent citizens are expecting. Then I'll throw it back to you for a few opinions from the rabble. How's that sound?

Reporter-2: Bet you have more fun than I do. Say, why is it you're always up front and I get stuck with the mob in the rear?

Reporter-1: Kismet, Jimmy. Kismet. What's it like back there?

Reporter-2: You simply would not believe the odor. An extraordinarily motley crew. What about you?

Reporter-1: I'd love to see the labels on some of these tunics. And from the looks of the sandals and pouches, I'd say Gucchi has finally come to Nazareth. How are we doing for time?

Reporter-2: Five seconds and counting.

Reporter-1: Five. Four. Three. Two. One.

Reporter-2: You're on!

Reporter-1: Good evening, ladies and gentlemen of our television audience. Welcome to Saturday Night Synagogue Live. My name is M. Emmett Stevens from the Public Broadcasting System. Together with my British colleague and analyst from the B.B.C., J-Glenn Murray, it will be our privilege to bring to you what is shaping up as a most exciting event. We are here at the Asilomar Synagogue to bring you all another first. Jesus of Nazareth, who has caused such a stir these past few weeks throughout the district of Galilee, is about to make his first public appearance here in the synagogue of this sleepy little town. Some say it's the old story of "home town boy makes good." There is a sense of excitement and expectation. People from all over this area have gathered to hear what this young man has to say. J-Glenn, perhaps you'd like to give us some idea what to look for this evening.

Reporter-2: Of course, Emmett, he will be reading from the Scriptures. It will be interesting to see just exactly what text he does choose to read. Not a great deal is known about this person who only recently has been brought before the public's eyes. He is a young man wrapped in mystery. I must confess that I share some of the same excitement that is so very much in evidence in this building this evening. And who could tell us what to expect, this evening, better than the very people who have assembled to hear this Jesus of Nazareth? So back to you, Emmett, for the opinions of some of the people in the front of the synagogue.

Reporter-1: Thank you, J-Glenn. I'm here in the front of the synagogue surrounded by many of Nazareth's religious leaders as well as prominent citizenry. And I'm going to find out why they are here this evening and just what exactly they expect to see and hear.

You, sir. Would you please stand up and tell our home viewers exactly what you expect to hear?

Man-1:	Well, I'll have to be honest with you. I'm new to this community. I really don't know what to expect.
Reporter-1:	Have you heard much about this Jesus of Nazareth?
Man-1:	No I haven't. But I look forward to what he has to say. There are obviously others here who do know him and they are excited. Can't you feel it in the air?
Reporter-1:	Yes, indeed I can. Thank you, sir. I guess we shall see what we shall see, if you'll indulge my redundancy. And now let's hear from someone else. You, sir, why are you here?
Man-2:	Where do you expect me to be on the Sabbath?
Reporter-1:	Brief and to the point. Wouldn't want to tamper with religious taboos, as it were. Thank you, sir. And you, ma'am, why are you here?
Woman-1:	I knew him when he was a little boy. This is such a great day and we're all so excited for him.
Reporter-1:	And it can be seen in your face and heard in your voice. Thank you, ma'am. You, sir. What do you think of this Jesus' abilities?
Man-3:	To be quite honest, not much! I mean, after all, he's just a carpenter's son. Not that there's anything wrong with that. It's honest work! But he hasn't had much formal education. I really don't know what on earth he's got to say to us.
Reporter-1:	Thank you for your candor, sir. So everything is not "peaches and cream" here in the front, J-Glenn. Besides a mood of expectation, there is also a note of caution and reserve. But let's hear from some more of the townspeople. You, sir. Why are you here?
Man-4:	Because my wife brought me.
Reporter-1:	Have you heard some of the stories that have been circulating about this Jesus?
Man-4:	Well, you can't believe everything you hear.
Reporter-1:	And you, ma'am. Why have you come?
Woman-2:	It's a big day for our synagogue. I wouldn't have missed it for anything in the world.

Reporter-1:	Thank you, folks. Nothing new, but certainly representative of the mood of many down here in the front. What about you, ma'am? You look a bit distressed. What do you think about all of this?
Woman-3:	I think this whole thing has been blown way out of proportion. And I also don't mind saying that I think he's awfully young and inexperienced to be getting up and speaking to us.
Reporter-1:	Thank you, ma'am, for your frankness. I understand that there is a couple here who knew Jesus' parents. Would you two please stand up? What do you think about all of this, sir?
Man-5:	It's a very proud day for his family. I only wish his father were here to see him.
Reporter-1:	And you, ma'am. What are your thoughts?
Woman-4:	Well, I understand that his mother had a little trouble when she was younger. *(Reporter looks embarrassed. Husband signals "hush" to wife.)* But I wouldn't want to hold that against her son.
Reporter-1:	So, a husband who is proud for Jesus' family and a wife who is willing to let "sleeping dogs lie." I believe we have time for one more opinion before switching to the back. You, sir. I understand you're a long time member of this synagogue. What are you expecting to see and hear today?
Man-6:	I'm a little skeptical about the whole thing.
Reporter-1:	Why is that, sir?
Man-6:	Well, in Bible school he was always asking these annoying questions. He was a bit of a smart-aleck. I hope he's grown out of that.
Reporter-1:	Well, there you have it, J-Glenn. The range of expectations here up front and close displays a diversity and polarity of expectations. But now let's hear from you and some of the riff-raff in the back.
Reporter-2:	J-Glenn Murray here. And I sense a slightly different mood in the back of the synagogue.
Reporter-1:	What would you say the ambiance in the rear is, J-Glenn?
Reporter-2:	Well, I would say that the characteristic mood back here is your basic "early outcast" motif. One definitely senses the presence of scum. So without further ado, let's hear from some of the scum. Yes!

118

	Here's a little man sitting over in the corner. Pardon me, sir. What is your name?

Jack: Jack. Jack Horner.

Reporter-2: And why are you here, Jack?

Jack: I come here every week around this time on the Sabbath.

Reporter-2: And what are your expectations today?

Jack: Same as every week: a handout! I'm hungry. Somebody always sees me, feels guilty, and takes me home and gives me a free meal. I'm hopin' someone will do it again this week. Them's my expectations.

Reporter-2: Yes. Thank you. Thank you, Jack! I see someone else over here a little more well-fed. You sir, why are you here in the back?

Gentile: I'm a gentile. *(Crowd gasps. Even the other marginal types move away from the gentile as if he has a disease.)*

All: A Goy! A Goy!

Gentile: This is as far as gentiles can go.

Reporter-2: Yes, I see. A little bit of the masochist in us all, eh?

Gentile: No! I didn't come for myself.

Reporter-2: Then why are you here?

Gentile: I have a servant at home who is very ill. I love him very much. He believes this Jesus can help him. I'm waiting for a chance to ask this Jesus for help.

Reporter-2: We certainly wish you all the best. But just in case, what sort of flowers does your friend like? And speaking of flowers, I've spied what looks like one of the Roses of Sharon here in the back. Tell me, dear, why are you here?

Rose: I just came here looking for a little acceptance.

Reporter-2: Why don't you feel accepted?

Rose: Because of my job.

Reporter-2: Well, what exactly do you do?

Rose: It's night work.

Reporter-2: What kind of night work, dearie?

Rose: *(She shakes her hands and head embarrassedly.)* Ummmmm?

Reporter-2:	Ohhh, I catch your drift! Say no more. I do hope you find who or what you're looking for. *(A motley male smothers the reporter. He is trying to get on the camera.)* I say, can I be of some assistance, old chap?
Cousin:	Have you seen my cousin?
Reporter-2:	I beg your pardon?
Cousin:	Jesus of Nazareth!
Reporter-2:	You mean you're related? Oh Emmett, what a find! I've discovered one of his brothers, or as some Scripture scholars insist "cousins." Well, just exactly what do you expect this evening?
Cousin:	I hope they give him hell!
Reporter-2:	Why in the world do you feel this way?
Cousin:	He and John always had the popularity and publicity. Our side of the family got nothing. I worked very hard to become a certified counselor and yet they're all flocking to him. And besides that, it's my birthday.
Reporter-2:	Oh, I see. Not getting older, just bitter! And moving right along there's a rather demure young woman to my immediate left. Pardon me, madam, why are you here?
Lame:	I'm hoping this Jesus will heal me.
Reporter-2:	Just a general healing or did you have something particular in mind?
Lame:	I'd rather not talk about it.
Reporter-2:	You're not referring to that rather misshapen foot there? I guess that cuts down on dinner dates. And dancing's out of the question. Let me say this about that: Good luck! Well, that wraps things up back here with the scum. Now we'll switch our cameras to the front again and my American colleague, M. Emmett Stevens.
Reporter-1:	A hush has begun to descend over the crowd. Jesus of Nazareth has arrived and taken his place. He is standing now and coming to the front of the synagogue. Let's watch and listen.
Narrator:	And entering the synagogue on the sabbath as he was in the habit of doing, he stood up to do the reading. When the book of the prophet Isaiah was

	handed to him, he unrolled the scroll *(Jesus mimes this)* and found the passage where it was written:
Jesus:	The spirit of the Lord is upon me; therefore, he has anointed me. He has sent me to bring glad tidings to the poor, to proclaim liberty to captives, Recovery of sight to the blind and release to prisoners, To announce a year of favor from the Lord.
Narrator:	Rolling up the scroll he gave it back to the assistant. *(Jesus mimes this.)* All in the synagogue had their eyes fixed on him.
Jesus:	*(Jesus walks slowly and deliberately from the front of the synagogue to the back where the marginal types are. They express their joy with their faces as he walks towards them. They reach out for him. He stands in the middle of them and joins hands with them. Everyone else in the congregation has turned their heads to watch all of this. Jesus lifts his and the other people's hands high.)*

Today this Scripture passage is fulfilled in your hearing.

(Here Jesus motions to the people he has joined hands with to go down the side aisles. As they do, they open up the doors and windows. They return to the back and leave with Jesus. Reporter-2 has been swept up by Jesus also.)

Reporter-1: Well, there you have it, folks. A picture is worth a thousand words. And don't forget that you saw it all here. Jesus of Nazareth, in an unprecedented move, read from the Scriptures and then made his way to the back of the synagogue where he joined hands with a motley looking crowd. And now for some on-the-spot reactions to what Jesus said and did, let's go to J-Glenn Murray who is with Jesus and the riff-raff in the back. Come in J-Glenn. Ahhh, J-Glenn, are you there? J-Glenn? We seem to be experiencing some technical difficulty. Sometimes those marginal types are thoroughly irresponsible, damaging property and equipment. Let's try one more time. J-Glenn, are you there? Well, if there's one thing I'm sure of, it's that there are some people still here in the front of the synagogue. So I'm going to get some of their reactions. You, sir, what did you think?

Man-1:	I've never heard anyone speak with such authority. His words had the ring of truth.
Reporter-1:	Thank you, sir. And you, ma'am, you look a little disturbed.
Woman-3:	Disturbed? I'm incensed! Where does that brash young man get off talking to his elders like that? Who does he think he is?
Reporter-1:	As you can see, there are some strong reactions to what Jesus had to say. You, sir, what did you think of all of this?
Man-2:	I'm not quite sure what to think. I'm confused. I was moved and disturbed, excited and troubled by what he had to say. I'm going to have to chew on this for some time before I make up my mind one way or the other.
Reporter-1:	Thank you. And you, ma'am, what did you think?
Woman-1:	It was fantastic! I find it hard to believe that it all happened right here before my very eyes. He was inspiring! He spoke from the depths of his heart and touched mine.
Reporter-1:	Thank you, ma'am. You, sir, what's your reaction to all of this?
Man-3:	I think he's got a lot of nerve coming into this house of God and pulling a stunt like that! That takes real gall! He'd better not show his face around here again. We know how to deal with trouble makers.
Reporter-1:	Some pretty strong words, sir. But you look like you can back them up.
Man-3:	You're damn right I can!
Reporter-1:	And you, ma'am. You looked concerned about all of this. What did you think?
Woman-2:	I feel so embarrassed and sad for his mother and family. If he keeps this up he's going to break his mother's heart.
Reporter-1:	Thank you, ma'am. And you, sir. You look worried. How do you react to all of this?
Man-4:	I think there was real substance to what Jesus said. They were hard words to hear, but they needed to be said. My fear is that if Jesus isn't careful he's going to make some powerful enemies.

Reporter-1:	And you, sir?
Man-5:	Well, I was an idealist and hopeless romantic when I was his age too. He needs a little reality therapy! I think that when he's lived with the Romans for a few years, it will take the edge off of what he has to say.
Reporter-1:	And what do you have to say, ma'am?
Woman-4:	He's just like his cousin John, a little too zealous!
Reporter-1:	We are almost out of time. I think I can squeeze one more reaction into the program. You, sir, over there. What did you think about all of this?
Man-6:	Frankly, I found it disgusting! I have some serious problems with this man's theology. And he'd better do some genuine soul-searching and study before he comes before the ordination board.
Reporter-1:	There you have it, ladies and gentlemen. The reactions are all over the lot. But all of you out there have seen and heard for yourselves. Jesus of Nazareth: charismatic or charlatan, prophet or pretender, faith-filled or fraud? This we can agree on: he is a man of controversy and contradiction. And so, from Asilomar Synagogue, that's the way it is. This is M. Emmett Stevens saying thank you and good night.

Finis

Theme:	The person of Jesus or "Who do people say that I am?"
Scripture:	Luke 4:16-30 *(The spirit of the Lord has been given to me.)* or Isaiah 42:5-9;18-22 *(I have called you to serve the cause of right.)*
Props:	1. One Bible that the narrator will read out of.
	2. Two microphones: one for the front and one for the back.
Production Notes:	This dramatization was originally performed as ·part of a concluding liturgy for a Methodist Pastors' Conference in northern California.
	It is important to use both the front and back spaces in order to help create some of the dramatic tension. Depending on the size of the space you are

working in, use microphones that can help all hear the responses of the people in the front and the back of the "synagogue."

The "Men" and "Women" should be right in the pews of the congregation. They should be in ordinary dress to facilitate identification with the other members of the congregation.

Study Questions

1. What do you think Christ must have felt when he stood before all those people and said and did these things? Do you think it was easy or hard for him to say and do these things? Why?

2. Read from the Book of Isaiah, chapter forty-two, verses five through nine and eighteen through twenty-two. What does the phrase "the cause of right" mean? How does God call each of us to serve the cause of right? How does God take us by the hand and form us? Can we resist or refuse to be formed by God? How do we do this? What could it mean for us to be covenants of the people or lights of the nations? Where else in the gospels does Jesus talk about our being lights? In what ways could the images Isaiah uses of a people "trapped in caves" and "hidden in dungeons" apply to us? Who or what can help us in this situation? Explore and discuss.

3. What other images occur to you analogous to the images you experience in the passage from Isaiah? Who are the blind? How are they blind? How might we be blind? Who are the bound? How are they bound? Who or what binds them? Are we bound? In what ways are we bound? In what ways do we bind others?

4. Read the fourth chapter of Luke's gospel, verses sixteen through thirty. How has the spirit of the Lord been given to each of us? Reflect and share. What did the Biblical gesture of anointing mean? Has God anointed us? How and for what?

5. Who are the poor that Jesus talks about? How does Jesus bring the good news to them? What is the good news for them? In what ways do you experience yourself as poor? What is the good news that Jesus brings to you? What are some of the ways that we can bring the good news to the poor?

Will our actions speak louder than our words? Explore and discuss.

6. What did Jesus mean when he said that the Scripture was being fulfilled while people heard it? Is the Scripture Jesus quoted being fulfilled in our midst? How? What are some ways we can help realize the full meaning of Jesus' words in our classrooms, our homes, our churches and our world? Explore and discuss.

7. What are some of the expectations of the people in the synagogue? What are your expectations of God? What did you think of Jesus when he walked from the front to the back of the synagogue? Why were some people so angry? How do you think the people in back felt? What do the people in the front of the synagogue have to do in order to see Jesus when he walks to the back? Why does God refer to Israel as a "stiff-necked" people when they refuse to listen to God's words? What does conversion mean for Christians? Must people turn to God once or many times in their lives? How do you do this?

8. Read Mark's gospel, chapter eight, verses twenty-seven through thirty. Who do people today say Jesus Christ is? Reflect and discuss. Who do you say that Jesus Christ is? Reflect and share. How do Jesus' words and actions affect you or find expression in your own life? Explore and discuss.

How Creation Learned To Give Thanks

Cast: Narrator   **Child**
                                God   **Dance**

Cast:	Narrator	Child
	God	Dance
	Spirit	Song
	Drama	Sound
		Sight

Narrator: Long ago, before time began, before anything we know existed, before there was anything to see or hear or taste or touch or smell, there was God. Yes, hard as it is to believe, God was all there was. And one day God discovered that he was alone, quite alone. So God said to himself:

God: Self, this is the pits! I am going stir crazy! I have got so much going on the inside of me that I have got to let it out.

Narrator: And so, God decided to do something about his predicament. God began to reflect on his situation and realized how quiet it was. So God said to himself:

God: Self, silence is golden, but too much of a good thing could drive even me bananas! So, let us fill the silence with sounds. Let my spirit go forth and bring out of silence — sounds.

Spirit: Sounds?

God: Yes, sounds!

Spirit: Yeah! Great! Sounds, lots of sounds! Ehhh, what are sounds?

God: You know, high sounds, low sounds, creaks, roars, rustling of wind, chirping of birds, waves pounding

127

against shores, horns blasting, hands clapping, feet stomping. All sorts of sounds!

Narrator: And so, God's spirit moved on this first day through creation and drew out of all that was — sounds. *(Here the performers begin producing a variety of sounds.)* And God heard the sounds and said:

God: *(Puffs on a cigar with pleasure.)* You know something, I like it!

Narrator: And God was so pleased with everything that he heard, that he wanted more. So he thought to himself again.

God: Self, creation sounds great, but it looks terrible! We need something to brighten all of this up. We need some pizzazz, some imagination, something to showcase the beauty of all that is. We need some color.

Narrator: And so, God sent his spirit forth on this second day, instructing her:

God: Let there be colorful sights to be seen.

Spirit: Sights! Right! Far out! Sightssssssss. Ehhh, what are sights?

God: Dazzle the eye! Bring light from darkness! Create shadows, shades, hues, primaries, pastels. Dress all my creation in the colors of the rainbow. Make everything a dazzling sight to behold.

Narrator: And so, God's spirit swept over all creation with the delicate and sensitive touch of a painter's brush. She deftly dressed everything in the colors of the rainbow. And all that was, was beautiful to behold. And God saw the sight of his creation and said:

God: Farrrr Out! Now I like that!

Narrator: And God was pleased with all that he heard and saw. But after awhile he began thinking again. And he thought to himself.

God: Self, everything sounds good and looks great, but something is missing. Imagine what it would be like if all that was could move. Moving sights and moving sounds!

Narrator: And so, God sent his quickening spirit throughout creation on this third day, to teach everything that was how to move. And when God saw and heard everything he made moving, God said:

God: You know something, the longer I am at this, the better I get. Now you have got to admit, that is good!

Narrator: And on the fourth day, God started getting restless again.

God: There is something missing. I hear sounds, all sorts of sounds, but there is no rhythm, no beat, no song. That's it!

Narrator: Suddenly God realized what it was that was missing. And he said to himself:

God: I want my creatures not only to make sounds, but music, beautiful music.

Narrator: And so God sent his spirit through all creation instructing her:

God: Teach all of creation how to sing, for every creature should have a song.

Spirit: Song! Music! Great!

Narrator: But God, concerned about the spirit who had been working very hard these past days, said to her:

God: You do know what a song is?

Spirit: Songs? Say, heyyyyyy! I got rhythm. I got music.

Narrator: And so, the spirit of God drew out of creation — song. And when creation heard itself sing, it got caught up in its song and went one step further. Creation began to dance. *(Here a recorded song is put on and all the creatures begin some dance.)* And when God saw and heard all of this, he said:

God: I not only like it, I think it's going to be around for a long, long time.

Narrator: God and creation were so caught up in what they were doing that they sang and danced their way through the fourth day and well into the fifth. Suddenly, God took stock of all the great things that were happening and said:

God: Who is ever going to believe all of this?

Narrator:	And God thought to himself, late on the fifth day:
God:	This is simply too good to be lost or forgotten.
Narrator:	And then God hit on it.
God:	I know what I'll do. Spirit, go forth now and teach creation to tell the story of how everything came to be and how it learned to dance and sing, and how it became beautiful to hear and behold.
Narrator:	And so, the spirit raced through creation and taught them all to dramatize, to tell the story with and without words. *(All creatures do dramatic gestures.)* And God saw all of this and he smiled. Then he said:
God:	Some might say I'm a bit biased in this matter, but I like this. I really like this!
Narrator:	And God was right on both counts. What he saw and heard, stories sung and danced, moved, spoken and mimed, all of them were pleasing to the ear and beautiful to the eye. Everything was very good. But, then again, there is nothing God loves better than a well-told story, *(God looks at the narrator and holds up his cigar.)* except, perhaps, a good five cent cigar! *(God smiles.)* But as the sixth day dawned, God became troubled. As he watched and listened to all the beautiful stories unfold, a tear came to his eye. God realized that as beautiful as all the stories were, there was no one to tell them to. There was no one who could appreciate them as he did. So God thought to himself:
God:	Self, there is still one thing missing. And that is someone to be filled with wonder at all that I have made. I need someone to share all these sights and sounds, this music and dance, these stories with.
Narrator:	God thought very hard on this. Who could appreciate and enjoy all that he had made as much as he did? And then God realized.
God:	That's it! Spirit, bring forth children! Let the child in everyone grow and marvel at the wonders of creation.
Narrator:	And so, on the sixth day, when God saw the delighted faces of children reveling in creation, he smiled at everything he made and said:
God:	How sweet it is!

130

Narrator:	And on the seventh day, God rested. He spent the day looking long and hard at all the beauty that surrounded him. And he was very, very happy. So all of creation basked in its beauty and rested with him. Early in the morning, on the eighth day, while God was still sleeping in, all of creation gathered together.
Drama:	I suppose you wonder why I called you all together. I don't think I have to say how much we appreciate all that Mr. Big, good ole Number One, has done for us. If it weren't for him, well folks, God knows none of us would be here.
Dance:	Would you get to the point, drama? You have a tendency to ramble.
Drama:	Well, I was wondering if we could all throw some sort of surprise "thank you" party for old sleepy head. Our little way of saying "thanks" to you know who.
Sound:	Great idea!
Child:	We ought to give him something. A present! It's not really a party without a present or some kind of gift.
Narrator:	And so all of creation tried to think of something they could give God on the eighth day. They put their collective heads together and thought and thought. Then the child spoke up.
Child:	What about giving God an ash tray or a brand new tie?
Narrator:	But that suggestion was immediately dismissed.
All:	Forget it!
Narrator:	Then sight spoke up.
Sight:	What about one, huge, gigantic, see-you-through-this-life-and-into-the-next cigar?
Narrator:	Now everyone entertained this idea briefly, but then decided it would take too long to make it. So this suggestion was likewise dismissed.
All:	Forget it!
Narrator:	Next, both song and dance spoke up.
Song:	How about a bottle of "After-Creation" cologne?
Dance:	Or what about a bottle of our finest cheap Chianti?

133'

Narrator:	Well, needless to say, both of these suggestions were voted down. *(All creation gestures "thumbs down" first with one hand, then with the other.)*
All:	Forget it! Forget it!
Narrator:	So all of creation was in quite a quandary. Drama perfectly summed up their sentiments.
Drama:	You know what our problem is? God is simply the hardest person we have ever had to find a present for!
Sound:	Yeah! What do you give someone who has everything?
Sight:	Something to keep it in?
All:	Forget it!
Narrator:	Now God happened to overhear all of this, for as we all know, he knows all! Well, when God sleeps he always keeps one eye open. God was very happy with all his creation was trying to do. But they were stuck. And so, on the eighth day, God sent his spirit through all that was, and gave creation one final gift. He gave them the gift of memory. She reminded them who they were and all they had. Suddenly, amid all the vetoes to suggestions, the child spoke up.
All:	Forget it! Forget it! Forget it!
Child:	Hey, wait a minute!
All:	Wait a what?
Child:	Wait a minute! That's it!
All:	What's it?
Child:	Our problem!
All:	What's our problem?
Child:	We've forgotten!
All:	Forgotten what?
Child:	Who we are and all we have!
Drama:	You know, the kid is right!
Song:	What do you mean?
Drama:	Think for a minute. What's the best way to say "thanks" when you've been given a present or gift?
	Use it. Of course, use it!

Child:	We had simply forgotten.
Narrator:	And so, all of creation finally realized how they could thank God for what he had given them. Armed with this knowledge, they roused him from his sleep. And on the eighth day, creation declared a festival of thanks. Sounds could be heard and sights seen. Songs were sung and dances moved throughout the entire day. Stories were told and children laughed and cried and clapped at everything that was seen and heard and felt. And towards the end of the festival, on the eighth day, God looked lovingly on all he had made and he smiled. Then he raised his hand to quiet all of creation. He stood and addressed them:
God:	Thank you, my friends. You couldn't have given me a more beautiful gift. You have made me very, very happy.
Drama:	Since this is your day, isn't there any one thing we could do, as a group, especially for you?
God:	Yes, there is. What I ask of you, my friends, is to remember this day and every day after, who you are and what you have been given. I ask you to tell the story anew in each generation, so that all of life may be a festival of thanks.
Narrator:	And you know, strange as it all seems, the story has not been forgotten. The festival continues and all of creation still knows how to do what it does best.

Finis

Theme:	Thanksgiving.
Scripture:	Genesis 1:1-2:4 *(The creation account.)* or Psalm 136 *(A Psalm of thanksgiving.)*
Props:	1. One big cigar.
	2. Some colorful cloth or banners for when God creates color.
	3. One recorded song for when creation begins to dance.
Production Notes:	This dramatization was originally performed as part of Modern Liturgy's First Annual Festival of the Lively Arts in Worship. It was commissioned by Modern Liturgy as part of the concluding

133

liturgy. Since the festival focused on liturgy and the arts, this dramatization brought together much of what had been happening during the day. Through this story drama we are invited to reflect on and rejoice in the gifts we have been given in the arts.

This story drama can be done as simply or elaborately as you wish. Let your imaginations suggest avenues of dramatizing.

Study Questions:

1. Have you ever felt like God does at the beginning of the dramatization? Why does God create? Why do you create? What are some of the ways you are creative?

2. Read the creation account in the Book of Genesis. Do you take the goodness of creation seriously? What would be some indications that you do or don't? Do you experience the goodness of creatures? Why or why not? Do you experience the goodness of the creation called yourself? Why or why not?

3. Psalm 136 is a litany of thanksgiving for creation. Think of all the creatures you enjoy. Name them. What do you like about them? Think of all the qualities you like about others. Name them. What is it that you like about these qualities? Think of all the aspects of yourself that you enjoy. Name them. What is it that you like about these qualities? How could you learn to like more of others and yourself? Explore and discuss.

4. How does creation finally decide to thank God? What do you think of their decision? How do you express gratitude in your own life? Do the creatures in the story drama give you any ideas of new ways to show gratitude for gifts in your life? What are the most important gifts in your life? Do you treat them as gifts? Why or why not? How do you share this gift of self with others? Explore and discuss.

5. Who is responsible for teaching creation how to give thanks in the story drama? Does the same spirit help the child in each of us to grow? How? What are some of the ways we can grow in our ability to wonder? How can we develop the ability to see and hear and experience creation freshly? Explore and discuss.

6. Was God pleased with creation's expression of gratitude? Why was God pleased? What did God ask of creation? Is it easy to remember who you are and what you have been given? Why or why not? What happens when you do? What happens when you don't?

7. Have you ever thought of your memory as a gift? In what ways is it a gift? Is it possible to be grateful for what we cannot remember? Why or why not? Jesus asked his friends at the last supper to "do this in memory of me." How do Christians fit the description of people who remember and give thanks? What do Christians remember? How do Christians express their thanks? Explore and discuss.

8. What is a festival? How can all of life be a festival of thanks? Would this be hard or easy? Why? How do we tell the story of God's love and God's gifts in our day? What are some of the ways other people and other generations have told this story? Explore and discuss.